LEARNING KINDERGARTEN MATH WORKBOOK

Kindergarten math activity book with counting, addition and subtraction practice, and word problems to prepare your child for 1st grade

Autumn McKay

Find me on Instagram!
@BestMomIdeas

Learning Kindergarten Math Workbook by Autumn McKay
Published by Creative Ideas Publishing

www.BestMomIdeas.com

© 2020 Autumn McKay

All rights reserved. No portion of this book may be reproduced in any form without permission from the author, except as permitted by U.S. copyright law.

For permissions contact:
Permissions@BestMomIdeas.com

ISBN: 978-1-952016-25-7

Table of Contents

Writing Numbers 1
Numbers and Counting 7
Skip Counting 28
Comparing Numbers 39
Addition 50
Subtraction 61
Measuring 72
Shapes 85
Calendar 96
Word Problems 107

Introduction

I'm going to use the pronoun he throughout the introduction, but please know I thought of your sweet little girl too as I created this book.

I'm so glad to be a part of your kindergartener's journey to learn math to help prepare him for 1st grade! It is my hope that you and your child have fun as he learns basic math skills. In this book you will find many activity pages to help your kindergartener master math concepts in an exciting way.

Early math exposure is a strong predictor for future success, not only in math, but also in reading and critical thinking skills. When a child is exposed to math early he is able to communicate more effectively using mathematics. For example, "I want 5 purple stickers" opposed to, "I want stickers." Learning math helps deepen an understanding of math concepts, vocabulary, and critical thinking skills. All of these skills help to develop a mentally organized way of thinking which can lead to better comprehension for reading—a child is able to organize the parts of a story to better understand it.

Here are a few tips and suggestions I recommend for using this book:

- First and foremost, have fun with your child as he is learning these math skills! The objective of this book is to help your child learn math, but also to build his confidence as he is learning new information.

- Sit with your child as he is working through the workbook. Read the directions together, offer guidance when needed, and be there to answer questions as they may arise.

- You are welcome to choose the order in which you would like to complete the book, but I do recommend focusing on one concept at a time.

- As you and your child are learning new math skills be sure to practice using them in the real world too. Count objects together, get a calendar for your child to mark off each day, make-up word problems for him to solve, and help your child to recognize numbers. This will help him to become more familiar with the new math skills he is learning.

- Feel free to contact me if you have any questions or concerns at Autumn@BestMomIdeas.com.

Most importantly, let your child have fun and enjoy the learning process!

WRITING NUMBERS

NUMBER 1-10

Say the number. Count the dots. Trace the numbers.

1 •	1 1 1 1 1
2 ••	2 2 2 2 2
3 •••	3 3 3 3 3
4 ••••	4 4 4 4 4
5 •••••	5 5 5 5 5
6 •••••	6 6 6 6 6
7 •••••••	7 7 7 7 7
8 ••••••••	8 8 8 8 8
9 •••••••••	9 9 9 9 9
10 ••••••••••	10 10 10 10 10

NUMBER 11-20

Say the number. Count the dots. Trace the numbers.

11 ••••• ••••• •	11 11 11 11 11
12 ••••• ••••• ••	12 12 12 12 12
13 ••••• ••••• •••	13 13 13 13 13
14 ••••• ••••• ••••	14 14 14 14 14
15 ••••• ••••• •••••	15 15 15 15 15
16 ••••• ••••• ••••• •	16 16 16 16 16
17 ••••• ••••• ••••• ••	17 17 17 17 17
18 ••••• ••••• ••••• •••	18 18 18 18 18
19 ••••• ••••• ••••• ••••	19 19 19 19 19
20 ••••• ••••• ••••• •••••	20 20 20 20 20

TRACE THE NUMBERS

Trace each number.

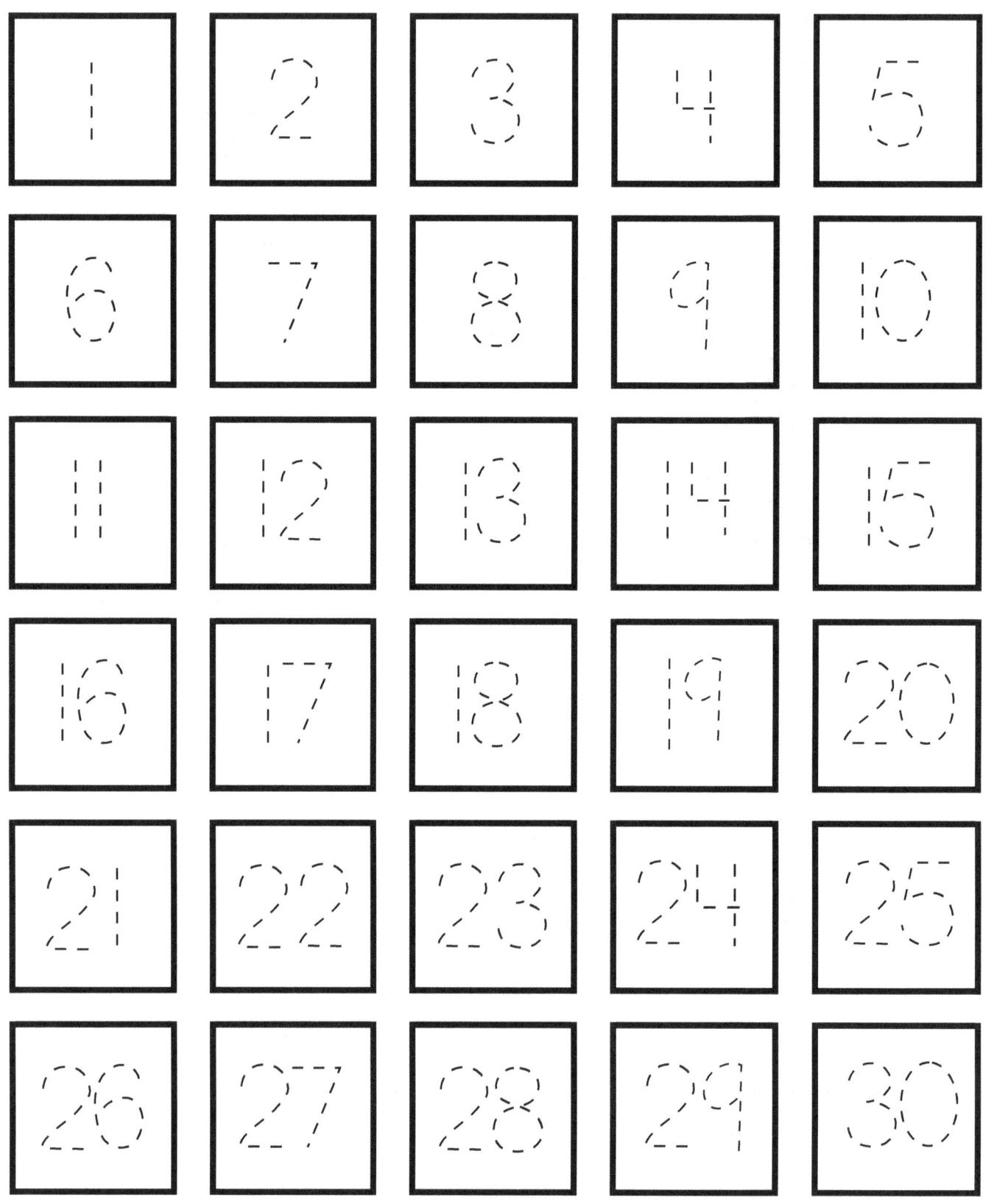

I CAN WRITE NUMBERS

I can trace the numbers 1-20.

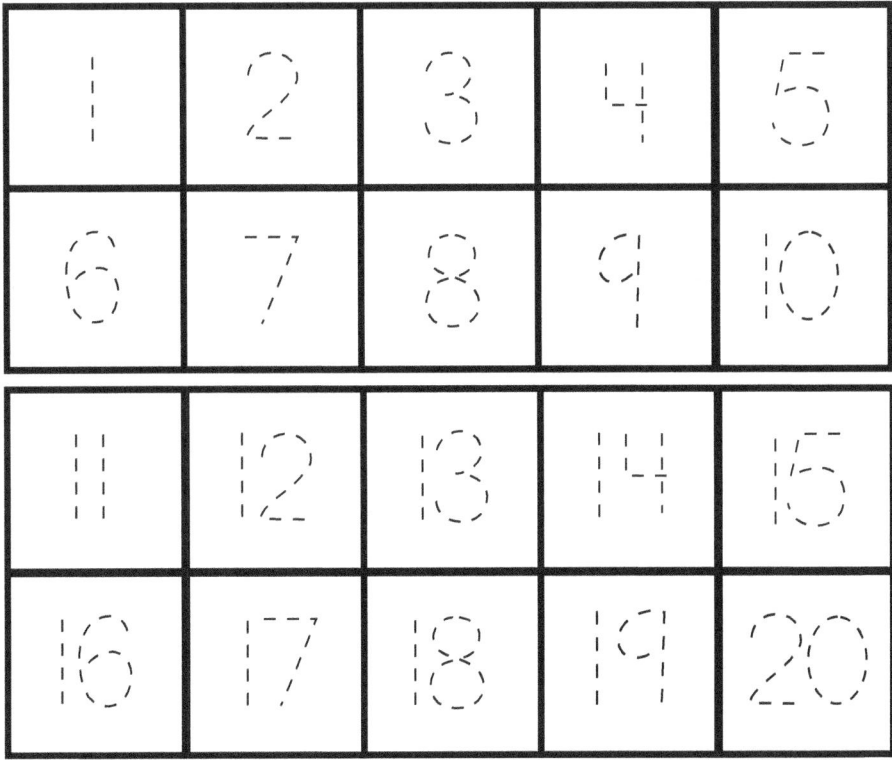

I can write the numbers 1-20.

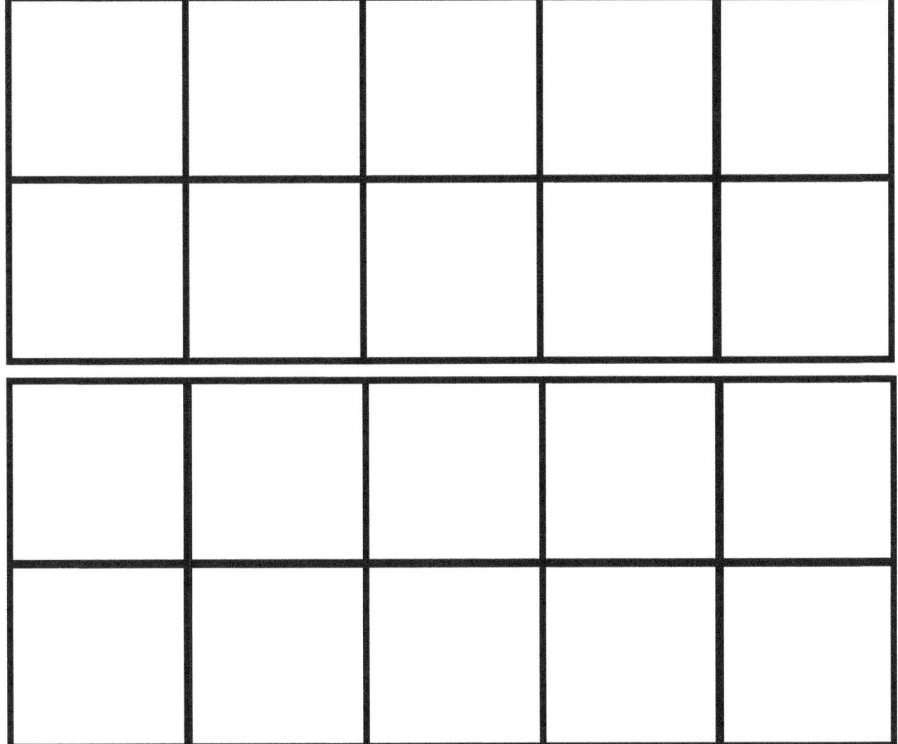

WRITE THE NUMBERS

Trace the numbers. Then use the dot to help you write the numbers on your own.

0

1

2

3

4

5

6

7

8

9

NUMBERS & COUNTING

NUMBER MATCHING

Draw a line from the number to its' name.

7	One
3	Ten
5	Seven
2	Three
0	Nine
8	Five
4	Four
9	Eight
10	Six
6	Two
1	Zero

NUMBER WORD

Color the correct number that matches the number word.

three	one	six
③ ② ⑩	④ ⑩ ①	⑦ ⑥ ⑤

ten	nine	four
① ⑩ ⑧	⑤ ⑨ ⑥	③ ⑤ ④

seven	two	five
⑨ ⑦ ⑥	② ③ ⑩	③ ④ ⑤

eight
⑧ ⑦ ③

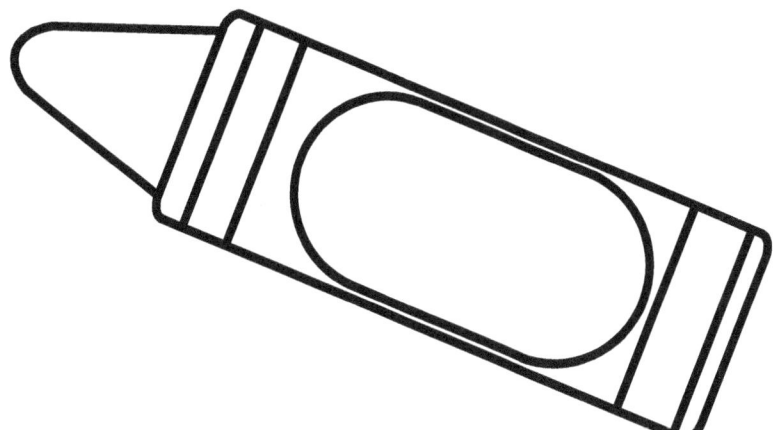

Learning Kindergarten Math Workbook | Autumn McKay

PRINCESS RESCUE

Can you help the prince reach the princess? Color a path from the prince to the princess by counting from 1-20.

COUNT AND COLOR

Use the number on the left to count and color the same amount of objects in the row.

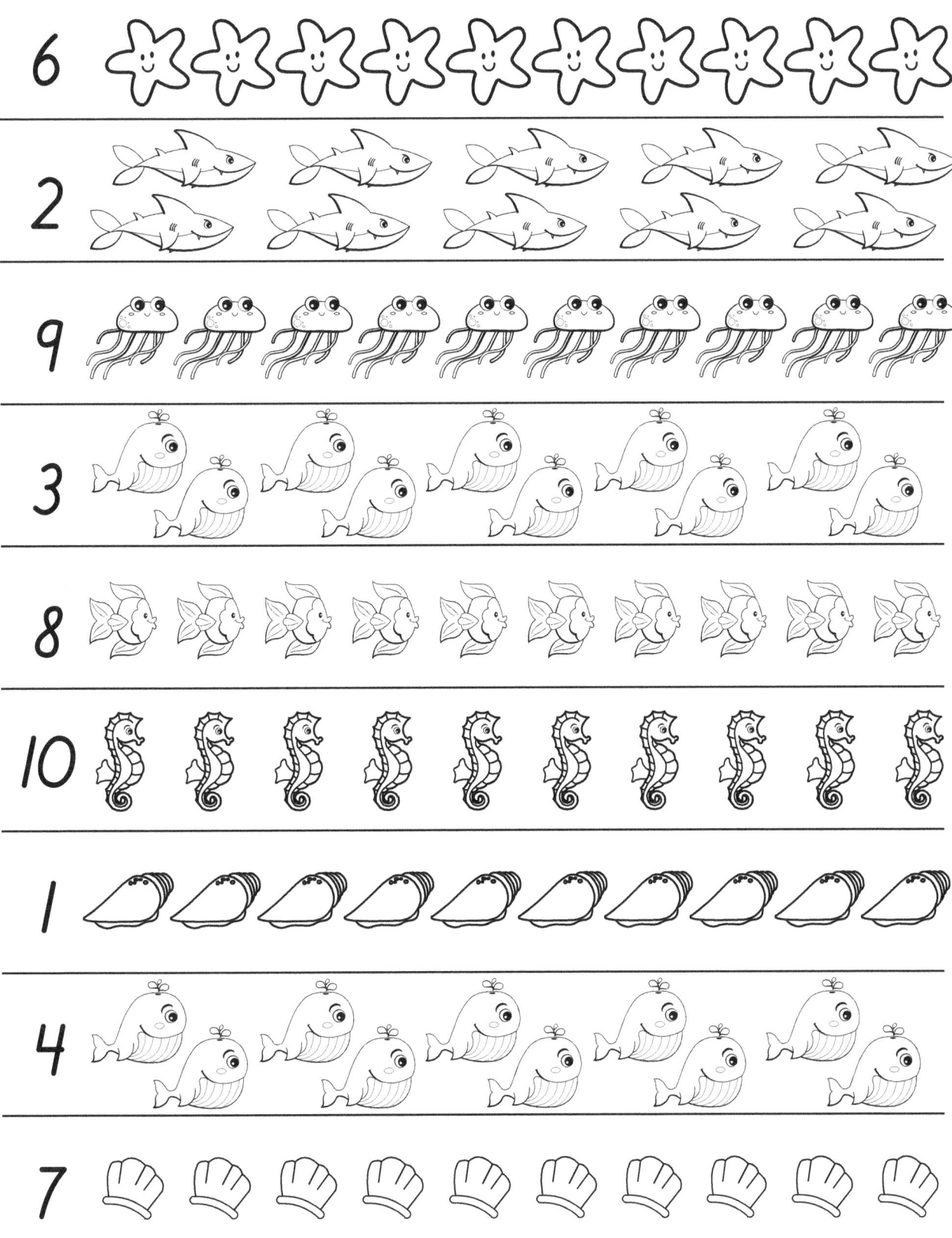

COUNT AND COLOR 2

Count the pictures. Circle the correct number. Color the ten frame to match the number.

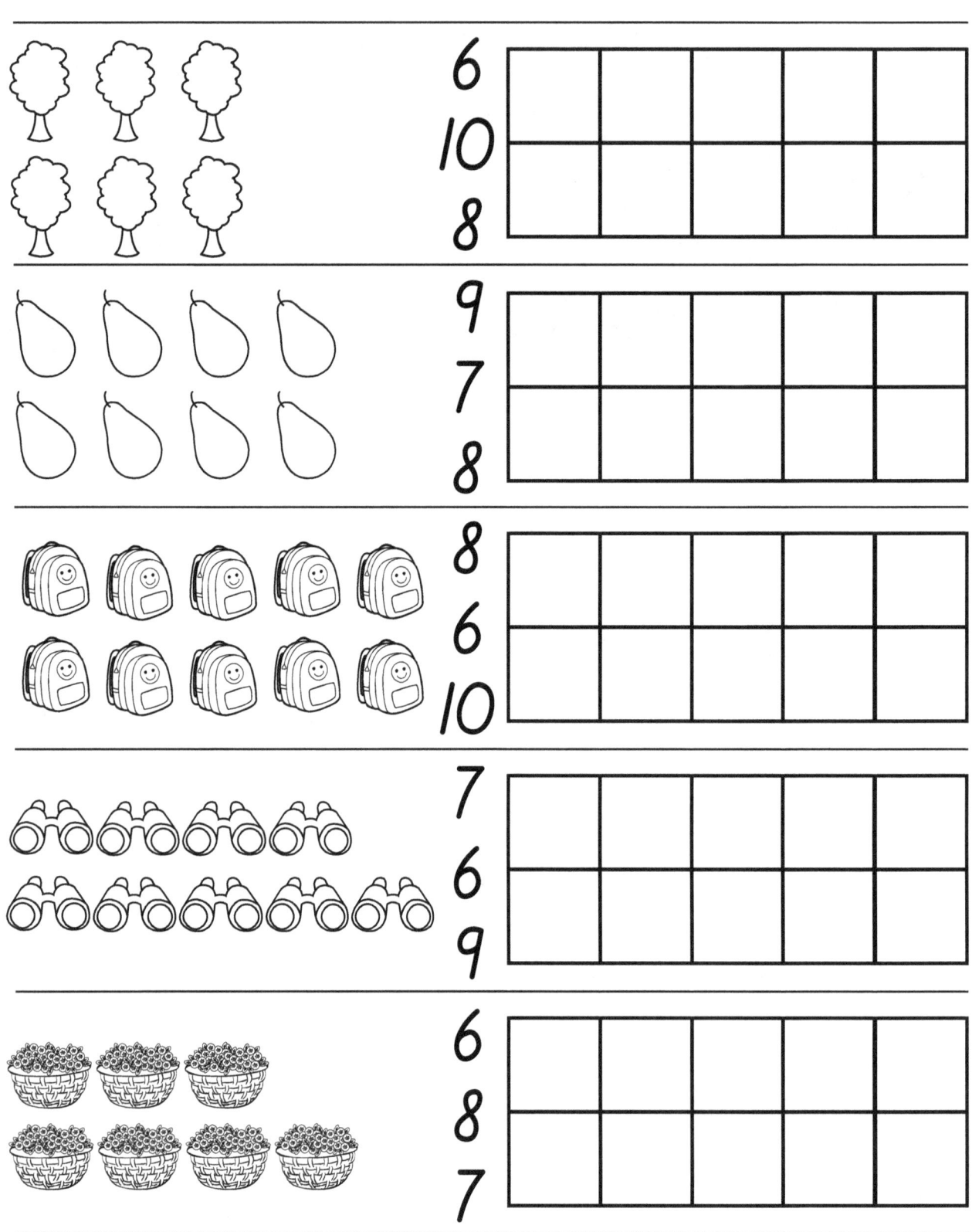

COUNT AND COLOR 3

There are many hidden sea creatures in the picture. Once you find a sea creature color it the correct color. Count the number of each sea creature and write it in the box.

HAT COUNTING

Count the hats. Draw a line from each number to the correct box. Color the pictures.

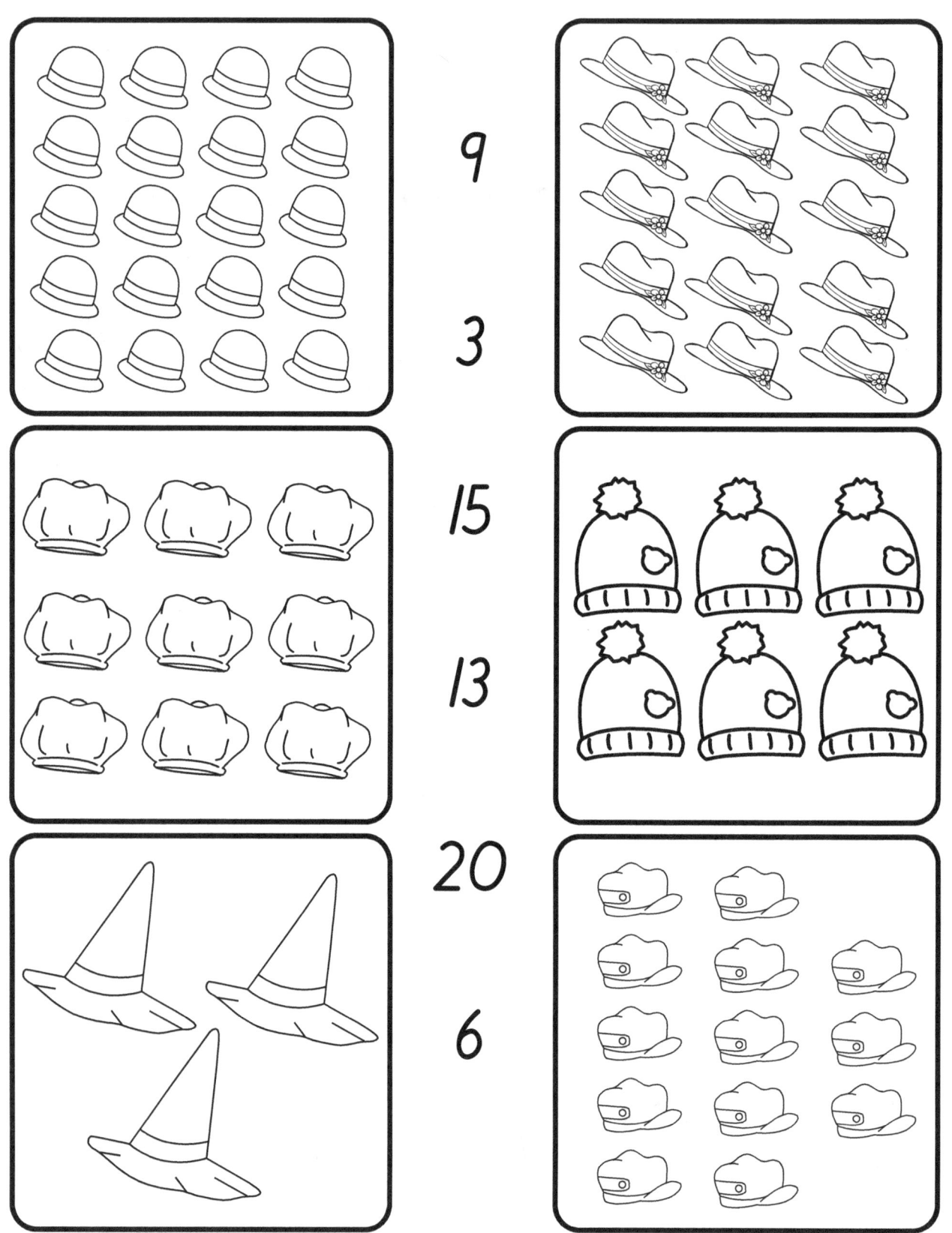

COLOR BY COUNTING

Count the number of dots to color the picture using the key.

5 orange   7 brown   9 purple
6 light blue   8 green   10 yellow

HOW MANY STARS?

Count the stars and write the number in the box. Color the stars.

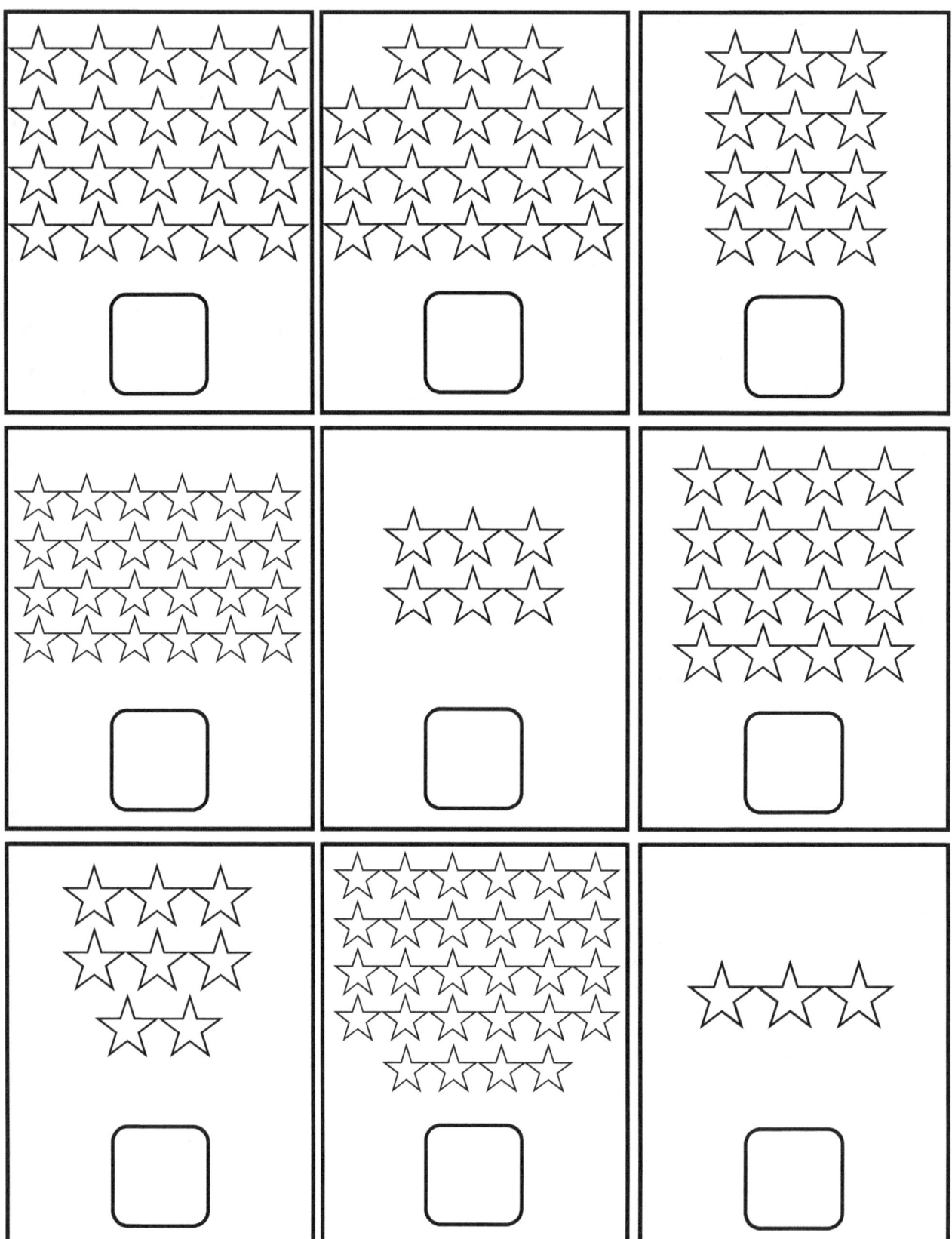

MONSTER TEN FRAMES

Count the number of filled boxes in each ten frame. Write the number in the box.

FILL THE TEN FRAMES

Use the number on the apple to color in the ten frame.

BUGGY TEN FRAMES

Color in the twenty frames with the correct number.

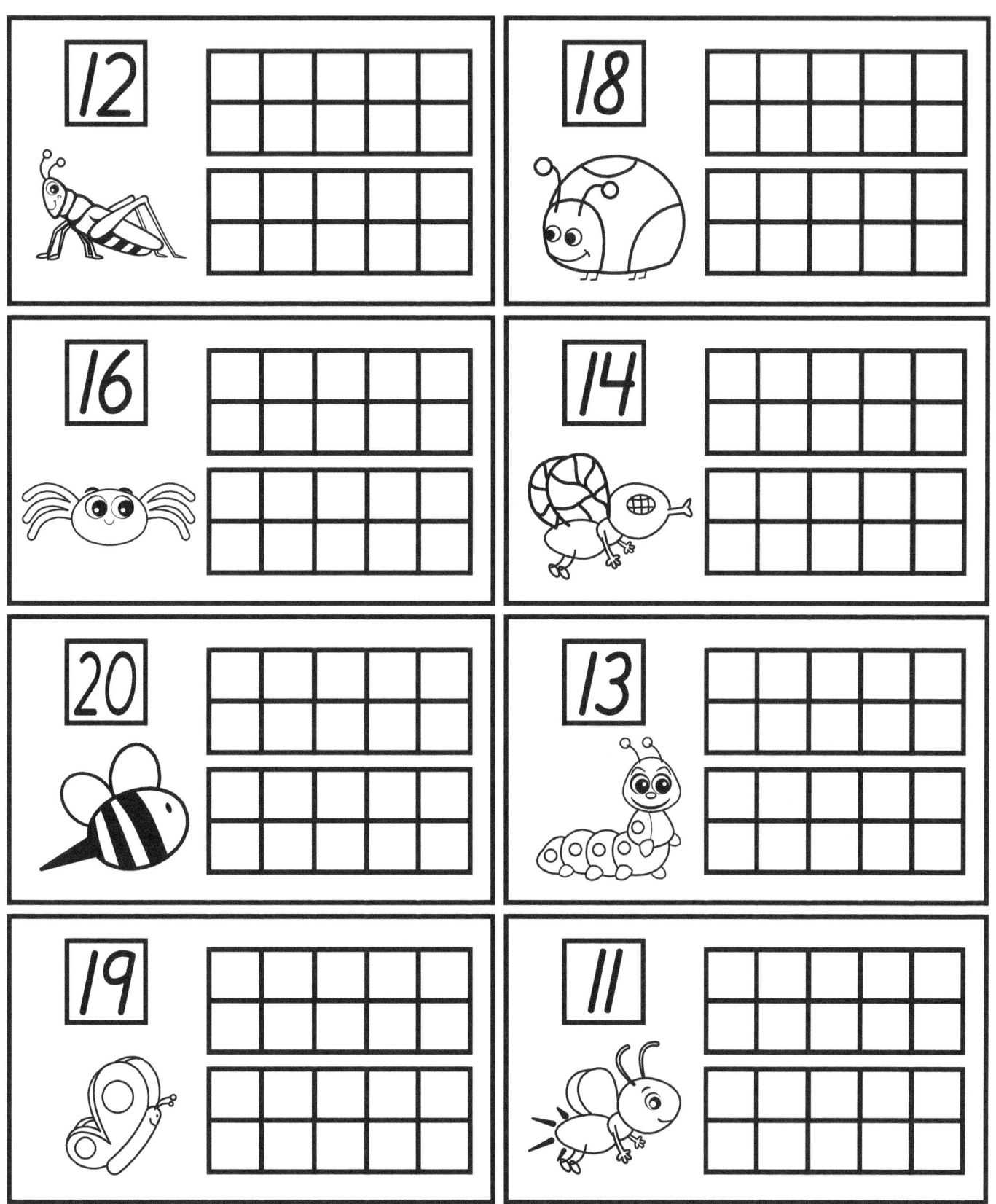

TEEN NUMBERS

Count the blocks and write the teen number on the line.

BASE TENS

Determine how many blocks are in each picture. Color the correct number.

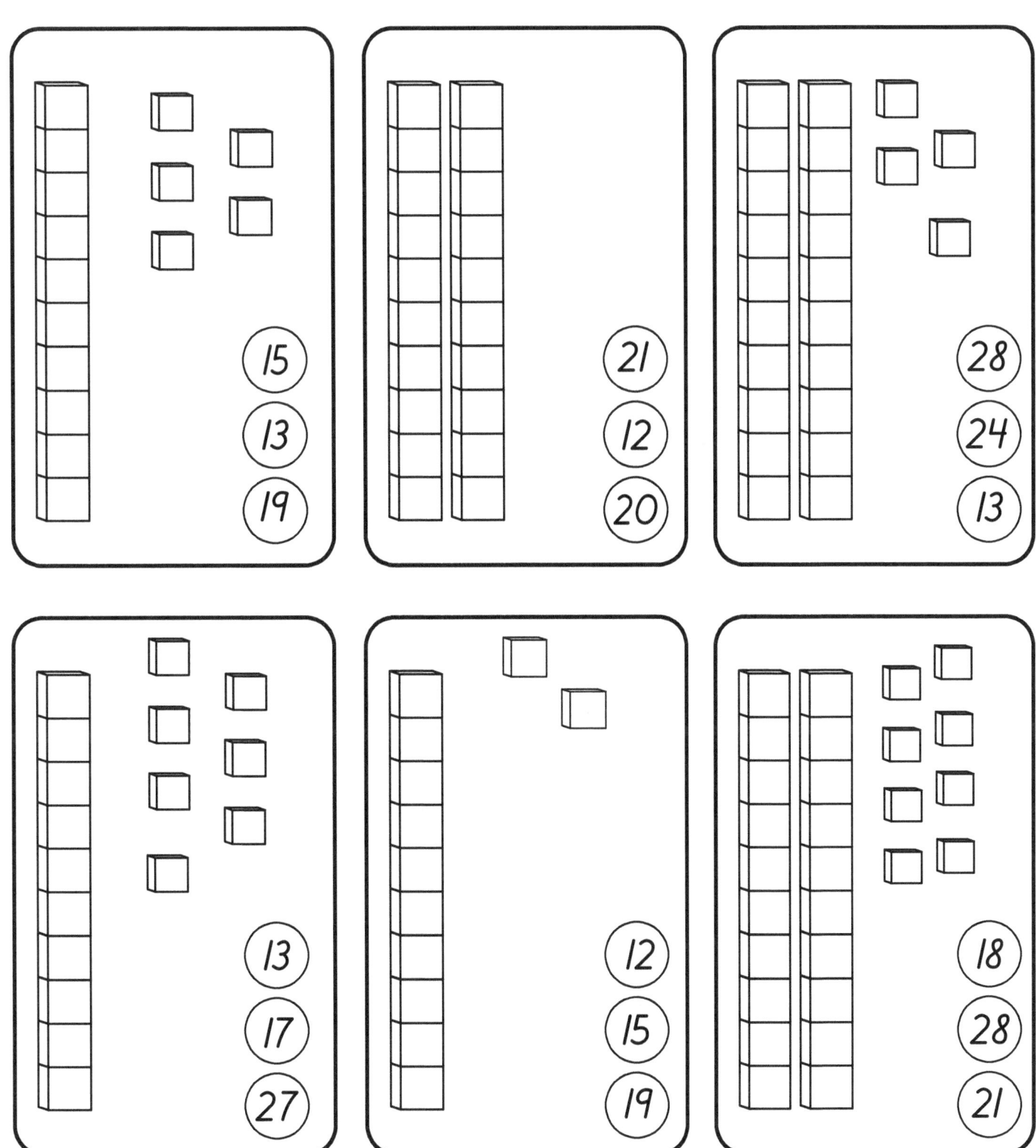

HOW MANY?

Count the shapes in each group and color the correct number.

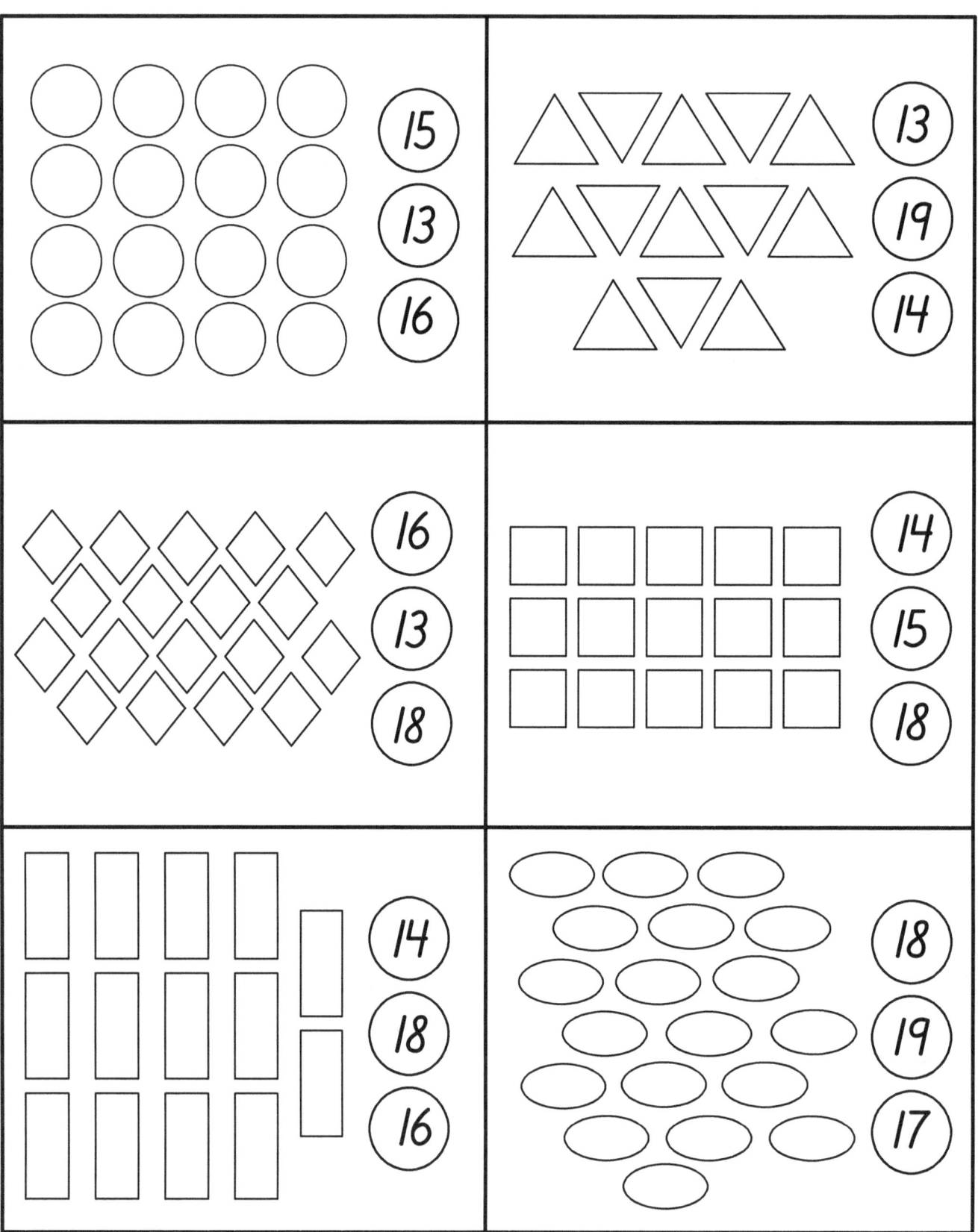

COUNT TO 100

Trace the numbers. Count to 100 by pointing to each number as you count.

1	2	3	4	5	6	7	8	9	10
11	12	13	14	15	16	17	18	19	20
21	22	23	24	25	26	27	28	29	30
31	32	33	34	35	36	37	38	39	40
41	42	43	44	45	46	47	48	49	50
51	52	53	54	55	56	57	58	59	60
61	62	63	64	65	66	67	68	69	70
71	72	73	74	75	76	77	78	79	80
81	82	83	84	85	86	87	88	89	90
91	92	93	94	95	96	97	98	99	100

Learning Kindergarten Math Workbook | Autumn McKay

MISSING NUMBERS

Write the missing numbers.

1			4		6	7	8		10
	12	13		15		17		19	20
21		23	24		26		28		
31	32		34			37		39	40
		43			46		48		50
	52		54		56			59	60
61		63		65		67			70
	72		74		76		78	79	
81		83		85		87		89	90
91	92		94			97	98		100

WHAT COMES NEXT?

Write the number that comes next in the blank.

14 ___	27 ___	89 ___
19 ___	40 ___	36 ___
16 ___	58 ___	44 ___
20 ___	62 ___	19 ___
13 ___	29 ___	80 ___
24 ___	33 ___	52 ___
28 ___	59 ___	86 ___

Learning Kindergarten Math Workbook | Autumn McKay

CARTERPILLAR COUNTING

Write the missing numbers on the caterpillars.

WHAT COMES BETWEEN?

Write the missing number.

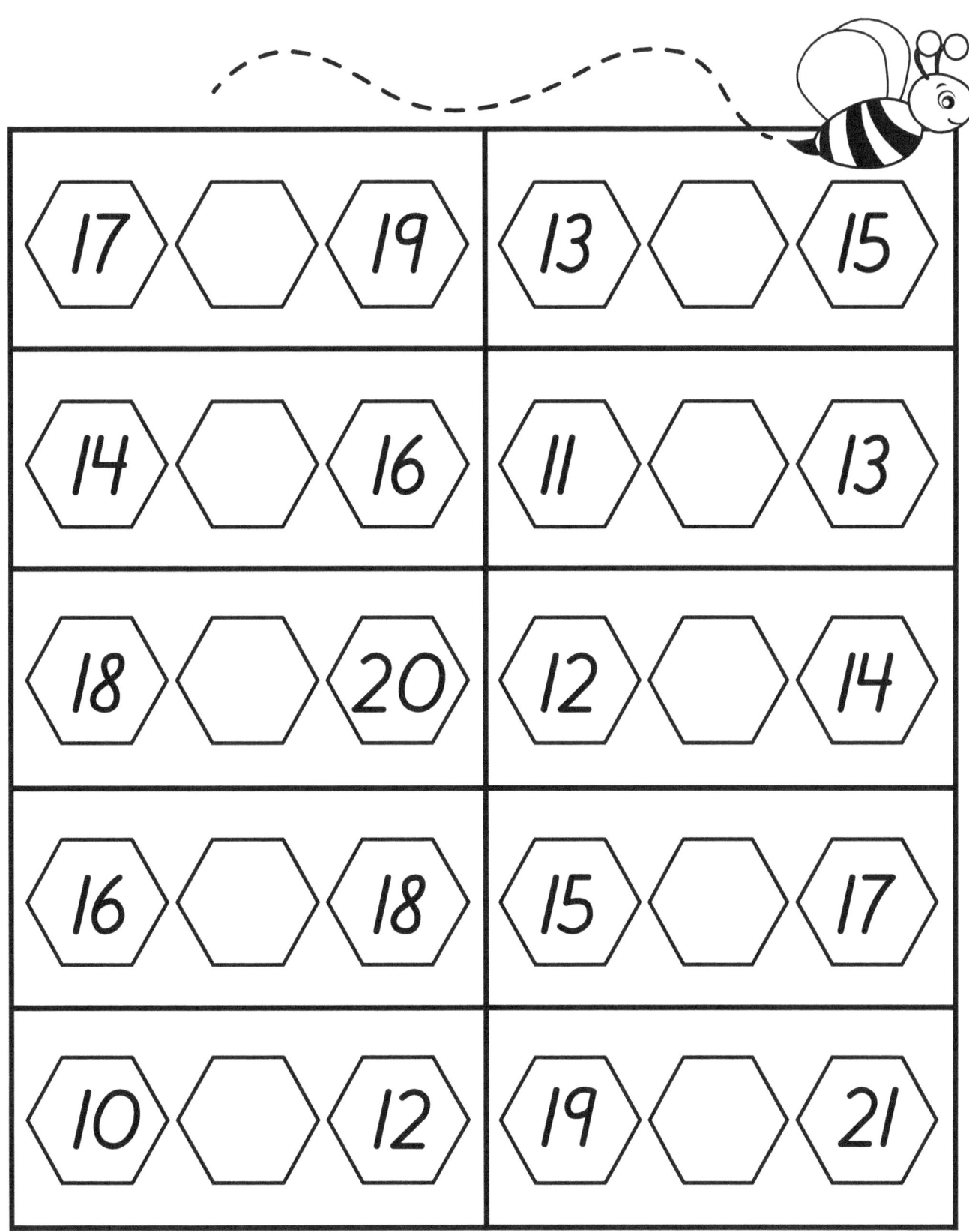

SKIP COUNTING

COUNT BY TENS

Count the tens. Color the correct number.

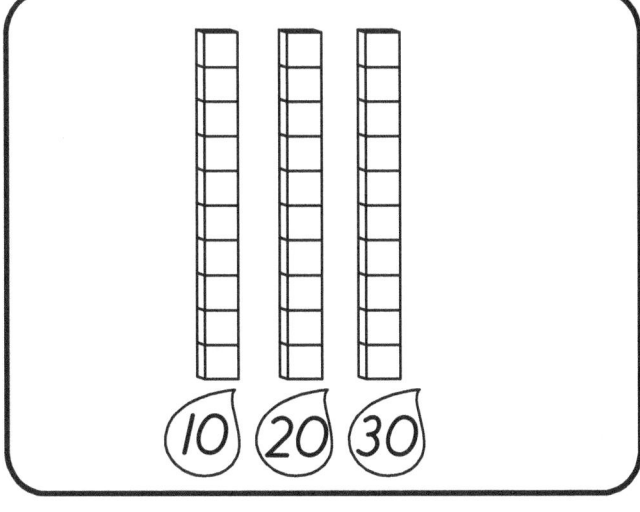

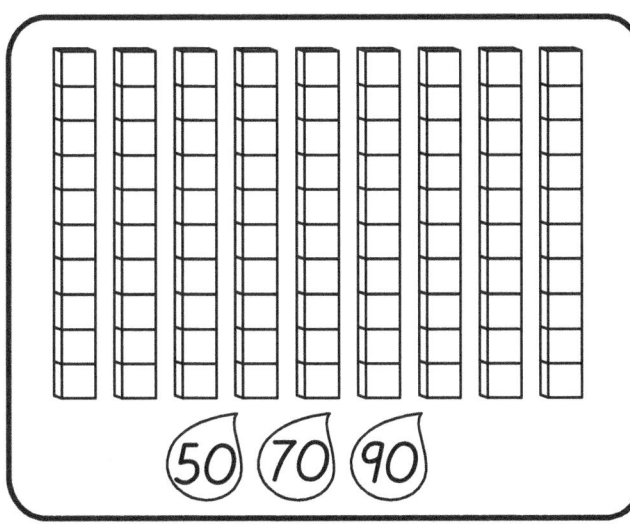
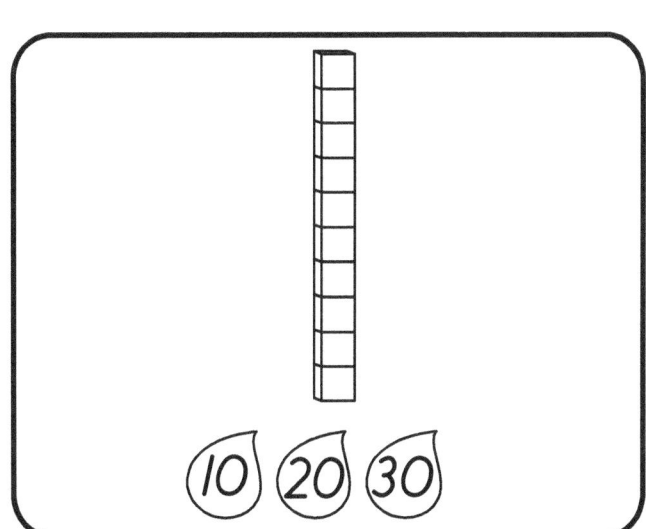

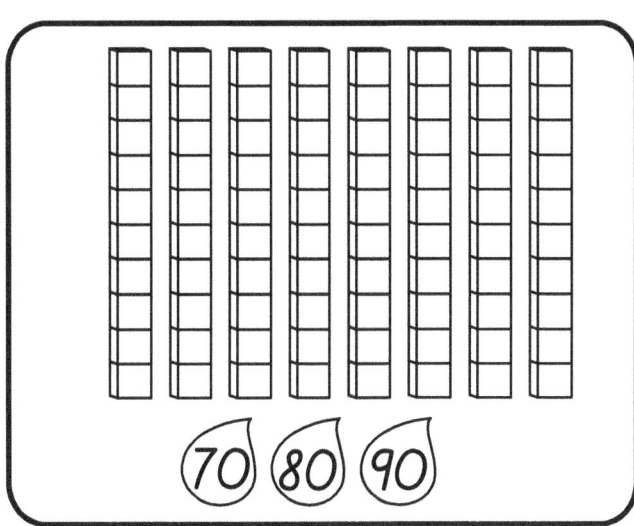

PENGUIN DOT-TO-DOT

Follow the dots to finish the penguin.

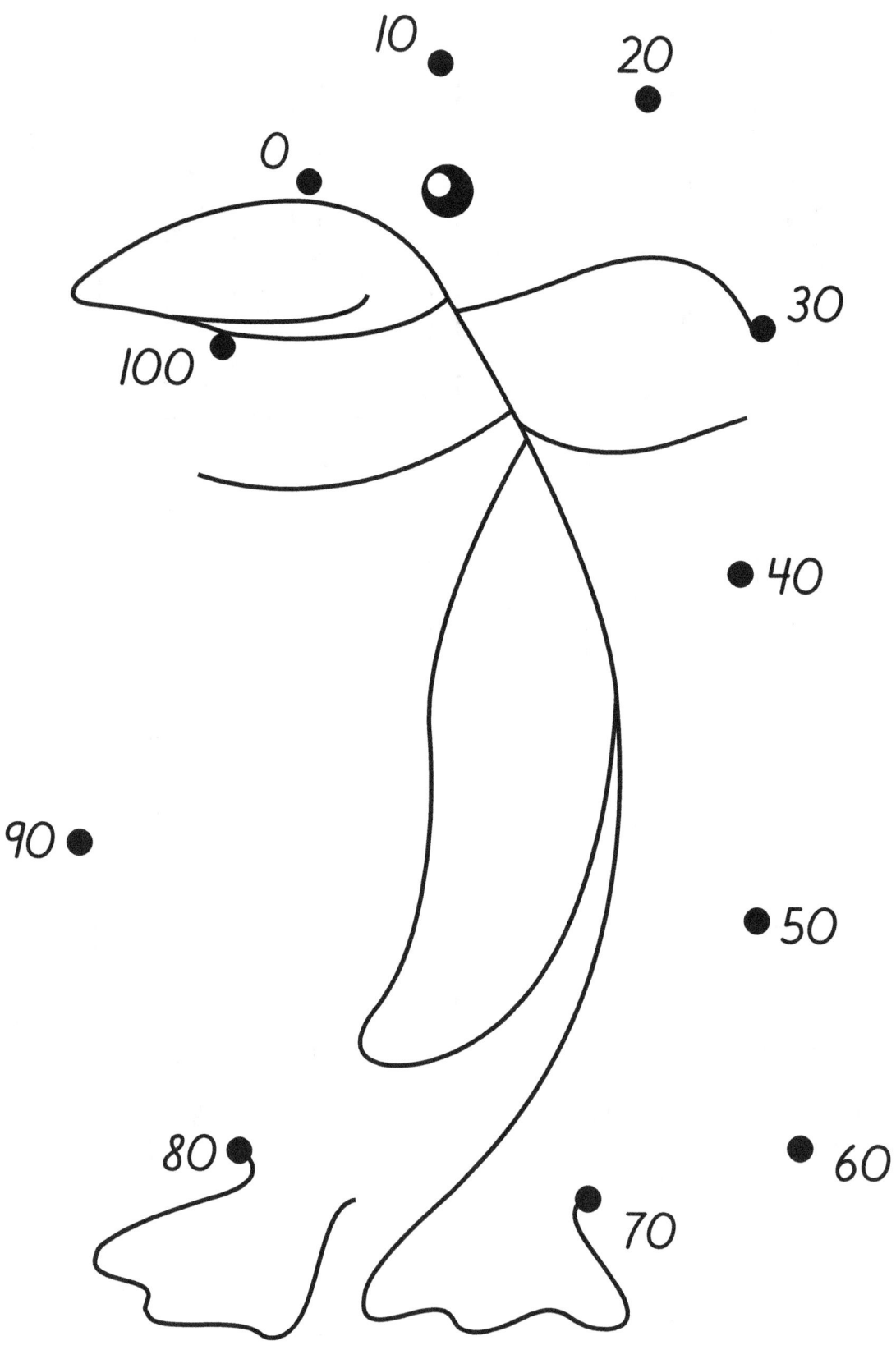

30   Learning Kindergarten Math Workbook | Autumn McKay

SKIP COUNTING WITH TENS

Skip count by tens. Color each number you say.

1	2	3	4	5	6	7	8	9	10
11	12	13	14	15	16	17	18	19	20
21	22	23	24	25	26	27	28	29	30
31	32	33	34	35	36	37	38	39	40
41	42	43	44	45	46	47	48	49	50
51	52	53	54	55	56	57	58	59	60
61	62	63	64	65	66	67	68	69	70
71	72	73	74	75	76	77	78	79	80
81	82	83	84	85	86	87	88	89	90
91	92	93	94	95	96	97	98	99	100

LEAPING BY TENS

Count by tens to fill in the missing numbers. Color the frogs.

LADYBUG MATH

Count the ladybugs. Write the missing numbers.

5 _ _ _ _

_ _ _ _ _

_ _ _ _ _

_ _ _ _ 100

DOG DOT-TO-DOT

Follow the dots to finish the doghouse.

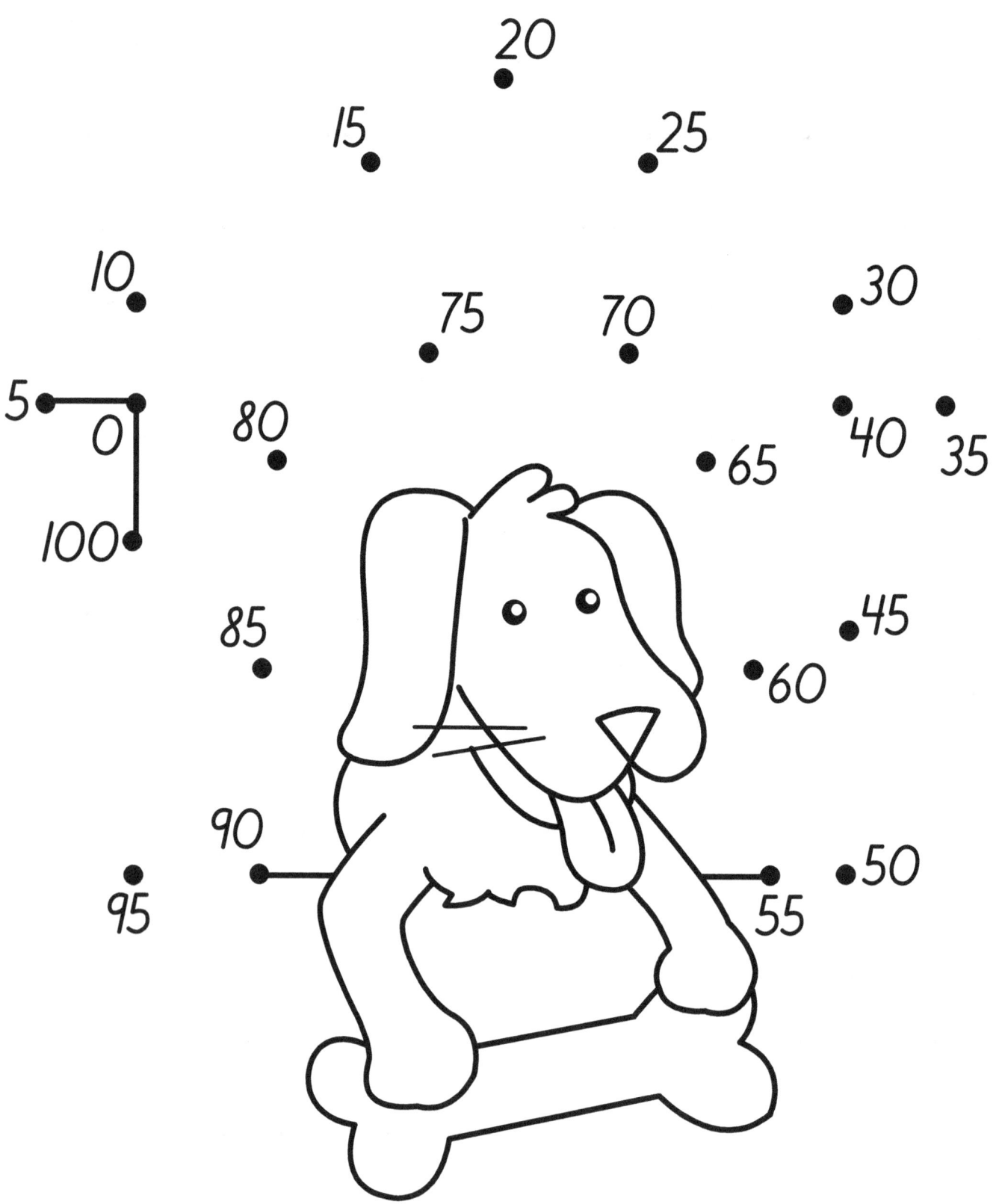

SKIP COUNTING BY FIVES

Skip count by fives. Color each number you say.

① ② ③ ④ ⑤ ⑥ ⑦ ⑧ ⑨ ⑩
⑪ ⑫ ⑬ ⑭ ⑮ ⑯ ⑰ ⑱ ⑲ ⑳
㉑ ㉒ ㉓ ㉔ ㉕ ㉖ ㉗ ㉘ ㉙ ㉚
㉛ ㉜ ㉝ ㉞ ㉟ ㊱ ㊲ ㊳ ㊴ ㊵
㊶ ㊷ ㊸ ㊹ ㊺ ㊻ ㊼ ㊽ ㊾ ㊿
(51) (52) (53) (54) (55) (56) (57) (58) (59) (60)
(61) (62) (63) (64) (65) (66) (67) (68) (69) (70)
(71) (72) (73) (74) (75) (76) (77) (78) (79) (80)
(81) (82) (83) (84) (85) (86) (87) (88) (89) (90)
(91) (92) (93) (94) (95) (96) (97) (98) (99) (100)

BUNNY EARS

Count the bunny ears by twos. Write the numbers. Color the bunnies.

2   4   6   8   10

 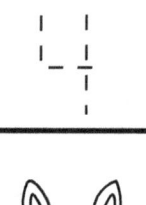  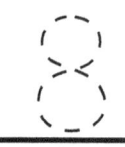 

ALLIGATOR DOT-TO-DOT

Follow the dots to finish the alligator.

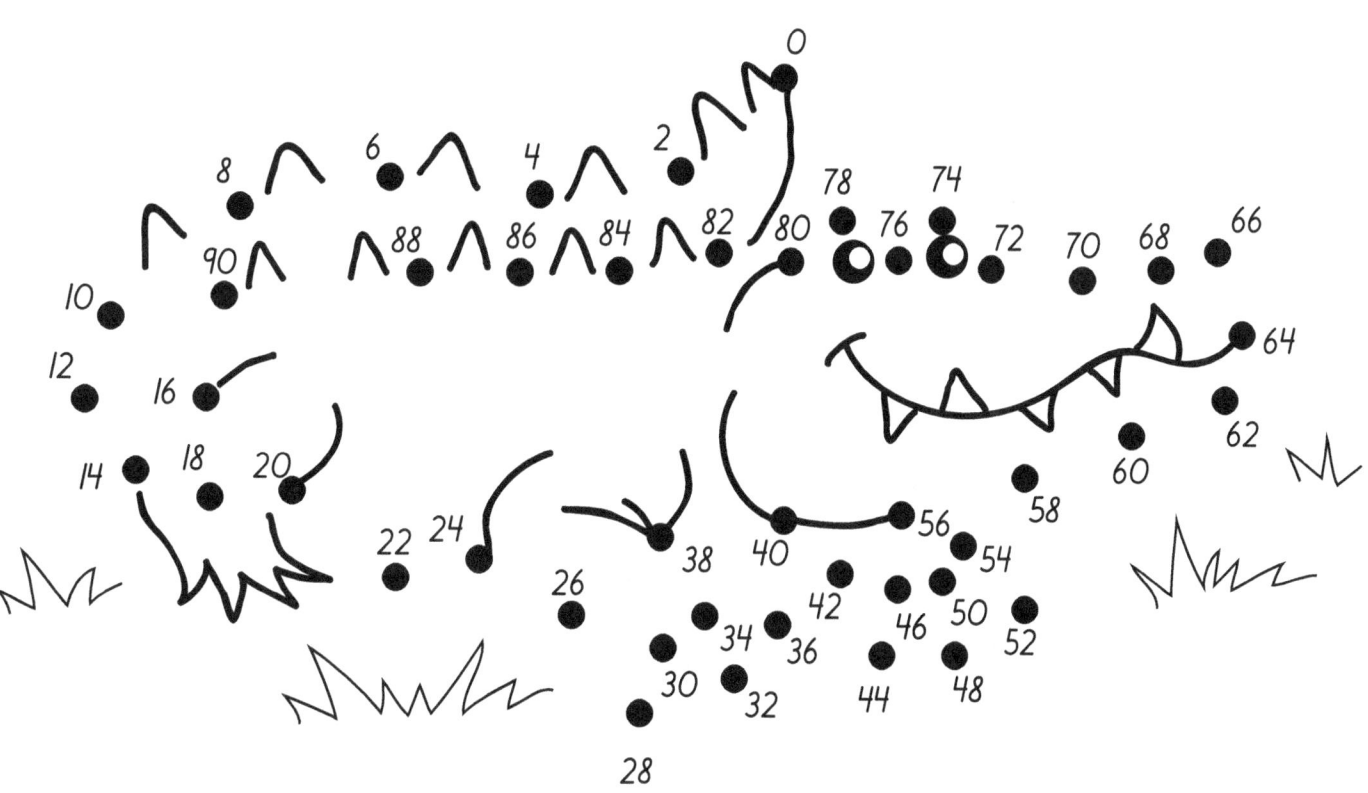

SKIP COUNTING BY TWOS

Skip count by twos. Color each number you say.

1	2	3	4	5	6	7	8	9	10
11	12	13	14	15	16	17	18	19	20
21	22	23	24	25	26	27	28	29	30
31	32	33	34	35	36	37	38	39	40
41	42	43	44	45	46	47	48	49	50
51	52	53	54	55	56	57	58	59	60
61	62	63	64	65	66	67	68	69	70
71	72	73	74	75	76	77	78	79	80
81	82	83	84	85	86	87	88	89	90
91	92	93	94	95	96	97	98	99	100

COMPARING NUMBERS

WHICH HAS MORE?

Count the apples. Write the number. Color the tree with more apples in each row.

WHICH HAS LESS?

Count the cookies. Write the number. Color the jar with less cookies in each row.

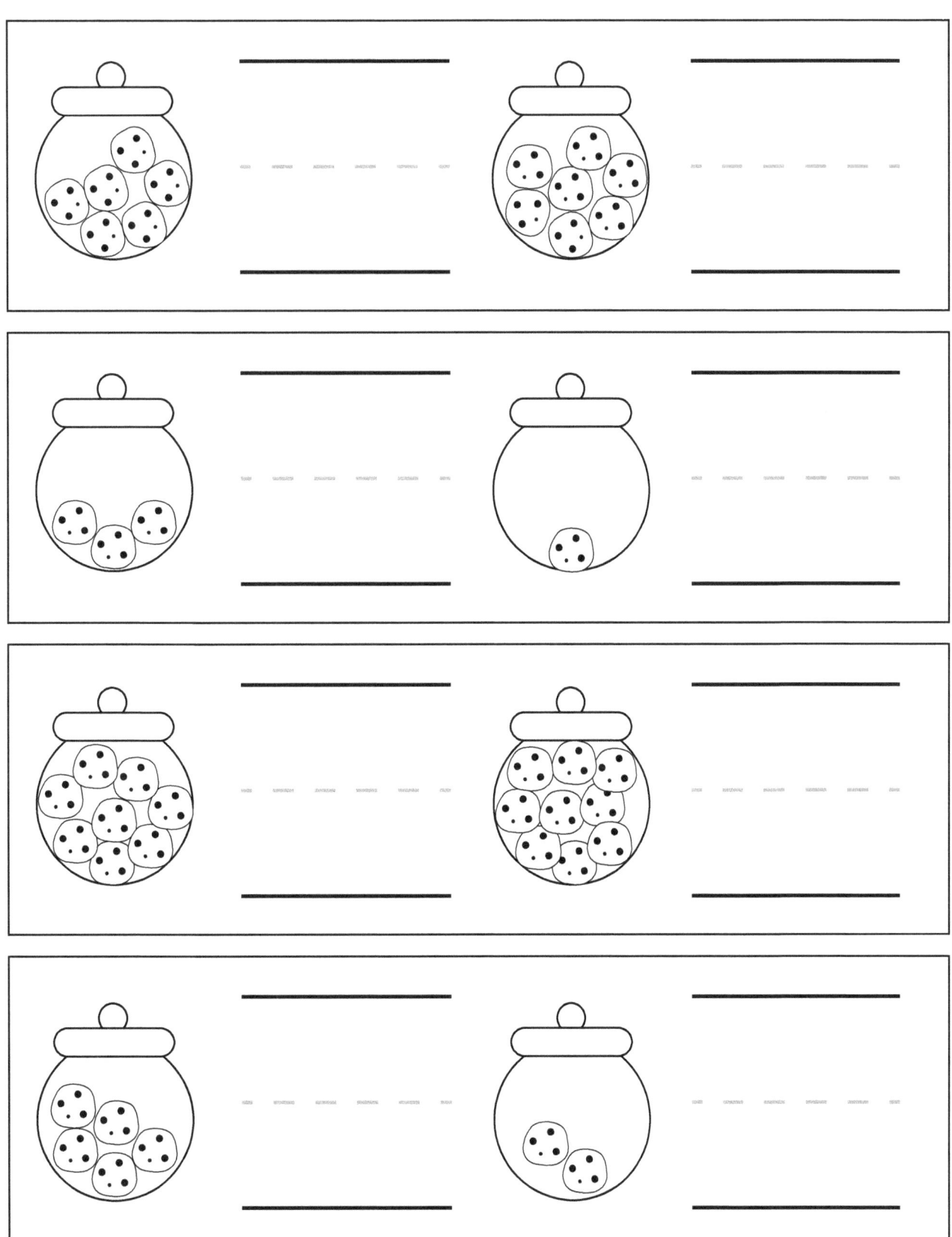

COMPARING NUMBERS

Compare the two numbers in each row. Trace more or less to complete each sentence.

MAKE THEM EQUAL

Draw sprinkles on the donut with less to make them equal amounts. Color the pictures.

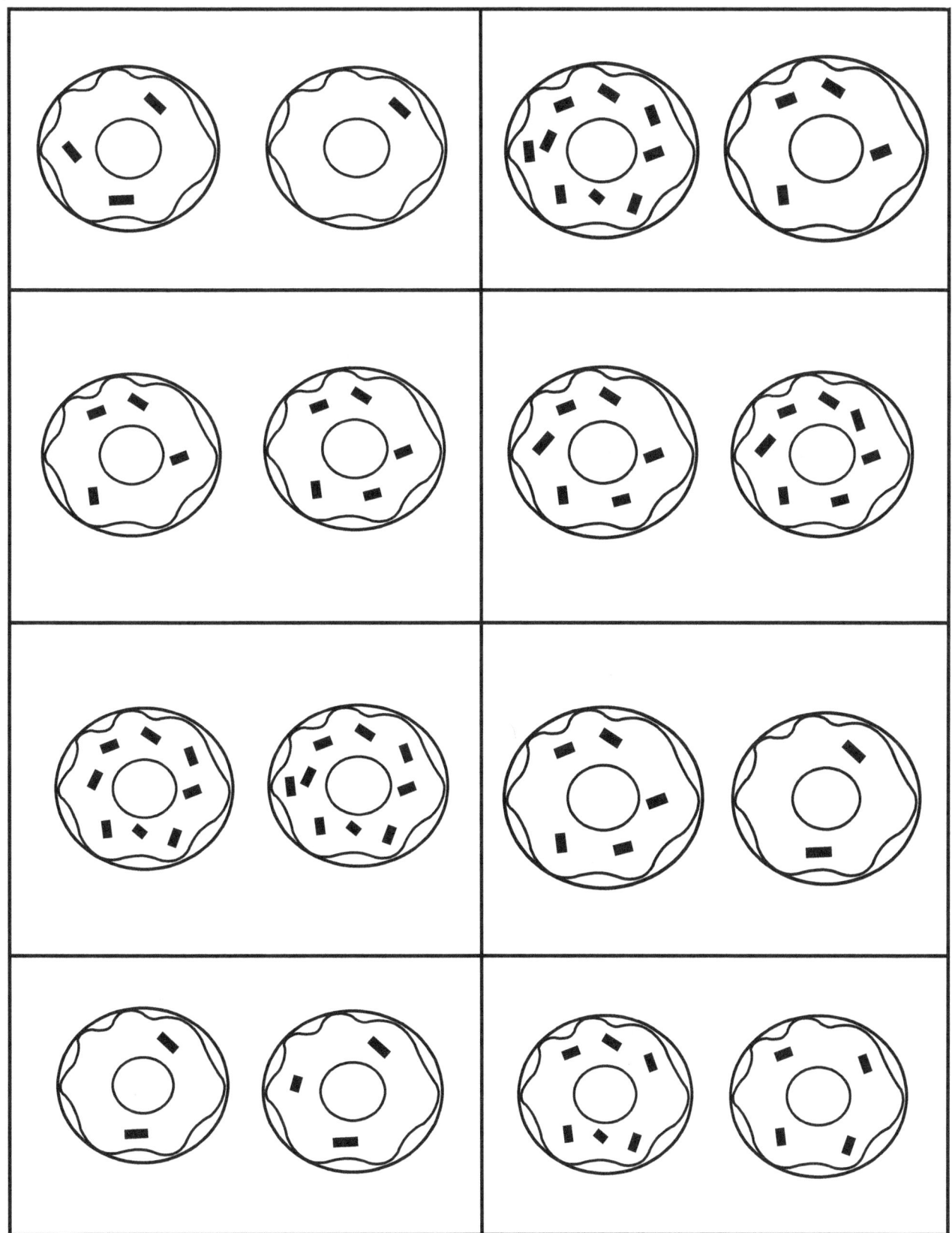

WHICH HAS MORE? 2

Color the gumball machine that has the most gumballs.

DRAW LESS

Count the seeds on the watermelon on the left. Draw less seeds in the watermelon on the right.

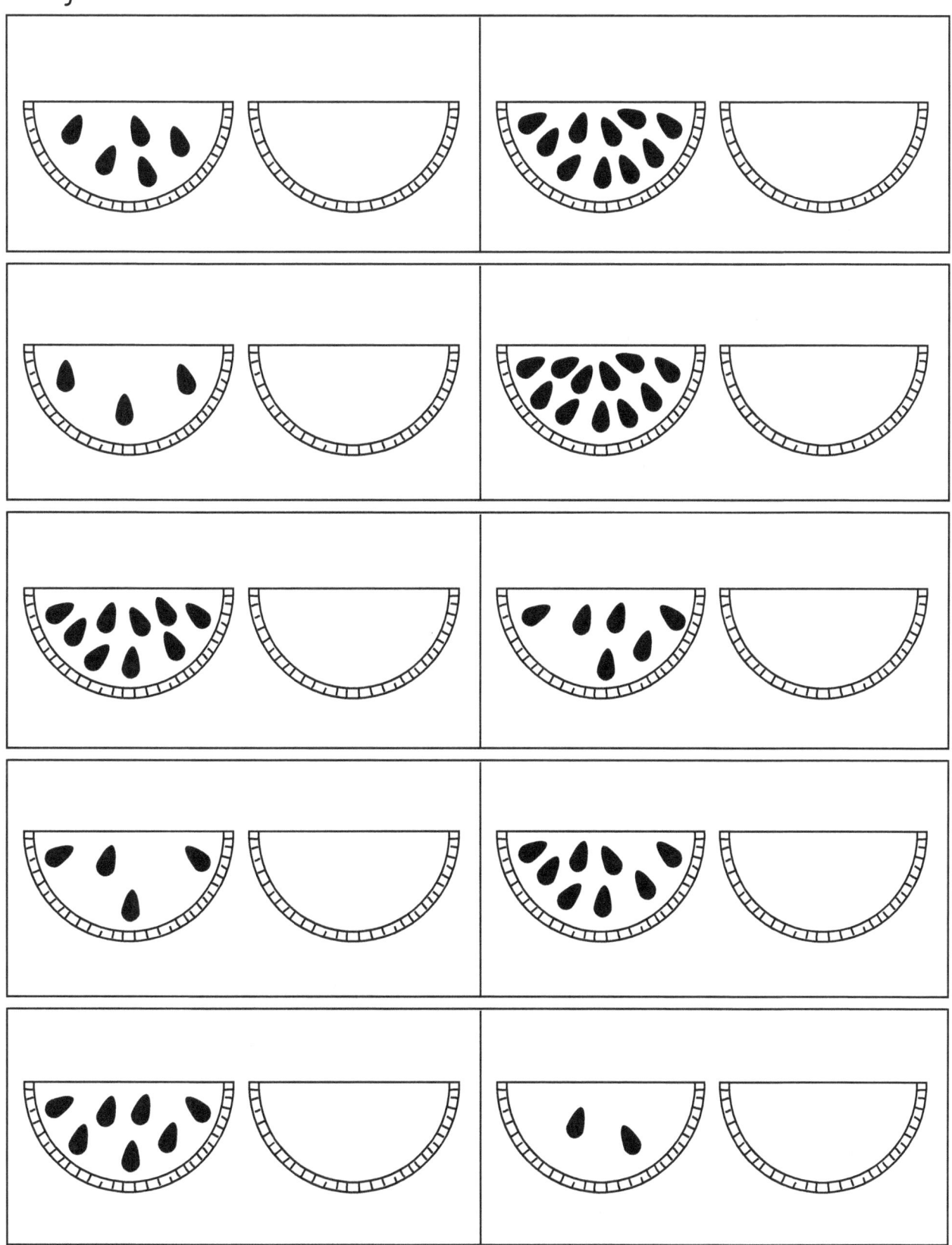

COMPARING DUCKS

Compare the sets of ducks. Color the duck that is greater.

ALLIGATOR COMPARING

Fill in each circle with the correct sign.

| > is greater than | = is equal to | < is less than |

10 ◯ 13	20 ◯ 5	4 ◯ 15
17 ◯ 5	15 ◯ 15	6 ◯ 1
12 ◯ 1	8 ◯ 0	18 ◯ 18
11 ◯ 20	14 ◯ 19	7 ◯ 17
3 ◯ 3	16 ◯ 2	9 ◯ 9

COMPARING FARM ANIMALS

Count the pictures and write the correct sign <, >, = in each circle.

COMPARING BALLOONS

Compare the numbers. Write, < or > in the circle. Color the greater balloon.

ADDITION

FINGER ADDITION

Count and add the fingers. Write the answer in the box.

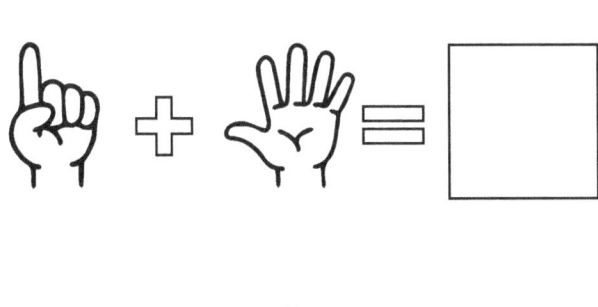

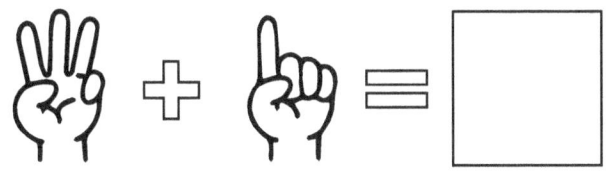

GUMBALL ADDITION

Draw the number of gumballs in each box to add the gumballs. Count and record the sum.

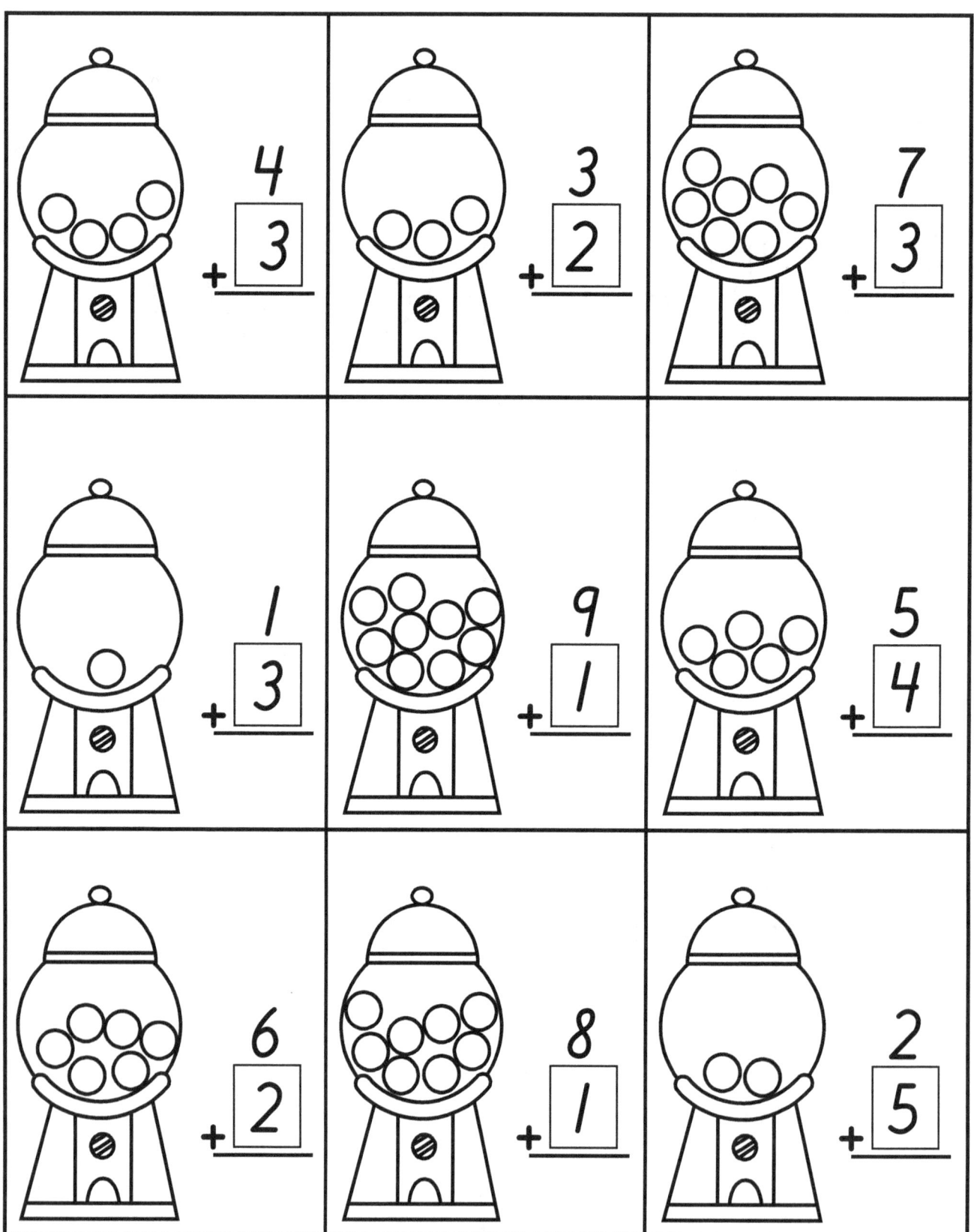

MAKE TEN

Draw more cupcakes to make ten. Finish the addition equation.

2 + _____ = 10

4 + _____ = 10

1 + _____ = 10

3 + _____ = 10

6 + _____ = 10

5 + _____ = 10

ADDING SNOWFLAKES

Add the numbers in the clouds. If you need help, count the snowflakes.

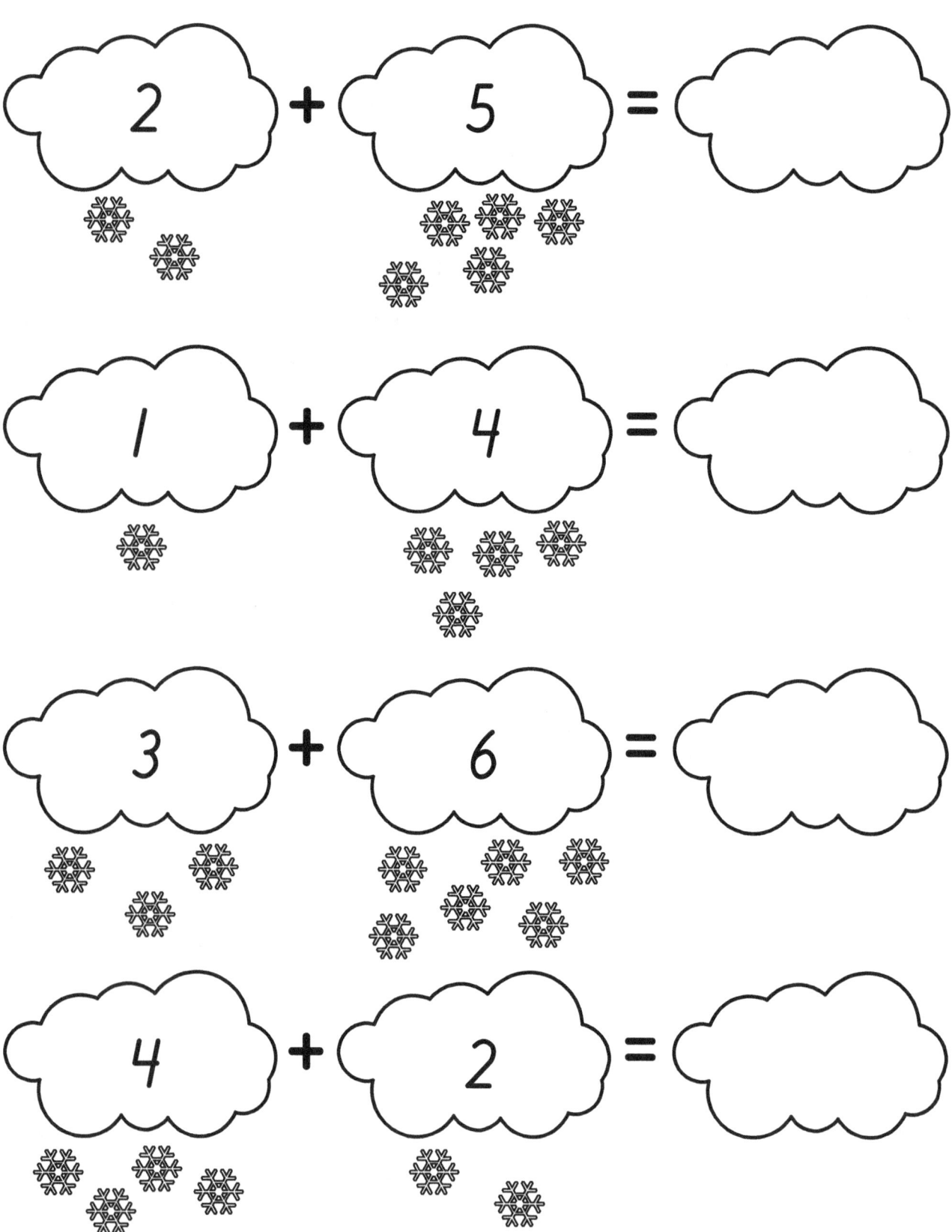

COUNT AND ADD

Count the number of turtles on each side of the addition sign. Write the numbers in the boxes and add.

🐢🐢🐢 + 🐢 = ☐3☐ + ☐1☐ = ☐4☐

🐢🐢 + 🐢🐢🐢 = ☐ + ☐ = ☐

🐢 + 🐢🐢 = ☐ + ☐ = ☐

🐢🐢🐢 + 🐢 = ☐ + ☐ = ☐

🐢🐢 + 🐢🐢 = ☐ + ☐ = ☐

🐢🐢🐢🐢 + 🐢 = ☐ + ☐ = ☐

🐢🐢 + 🐢 = ☐ + ☐ = ☐

NUMBER LINE ADDING

Use the number line to help solve the addition problem.

3 + 1 = __4__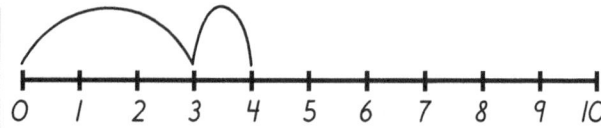

6 + 4 = _____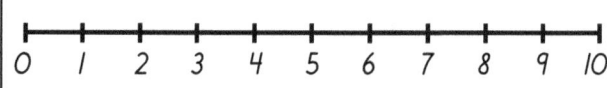

2 + 7 = _____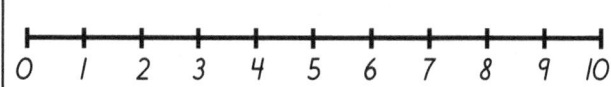

3 + 3 = _____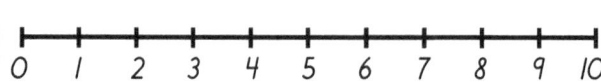

2 + 4 = _____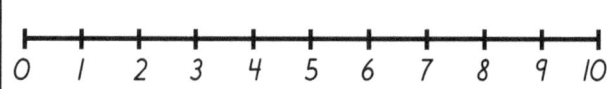

1 + 8 = _____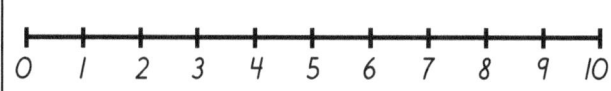

3 + 3 = _____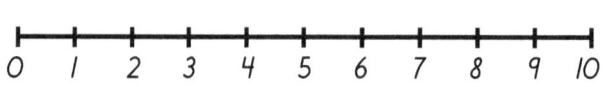

2 + 2 = _____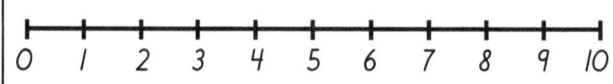

2 + 3 = _____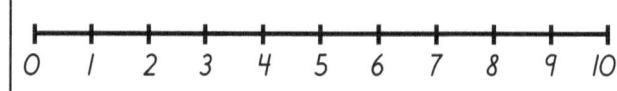

5 + 4 = _____

SNOWMAN ADDITION

Solve the addition problems. Count and color the snowmen.

2 + 8 =	3 + 4 =
2 + 0 =	5 + 5 =
7 + 1 =	3 + 2 =
6 + 3 =	1 + 1 =

COLOR AND ADD

Color the correct amount of apples for each addend. Solve the addition problem.

5 + 4 = ___	1 + 6 = ___
3 + 7 = ___	5 + 5 = ___
2 + 8 = ___	4 + 6 = ___
2 + 7 = ___	5 + 1 = ___
7 + 0 = ___	2 + 4 = ___

Learning Kindergarten Math Workbook | Autumn McKay

MANY WAYS TO ADD

Show all the ways to solve this problem.

Read
I see 6 whales
3 more swim by.
How many whales altogether?

Draw

Number Line

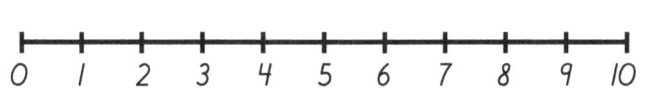

Color the Ten Frame

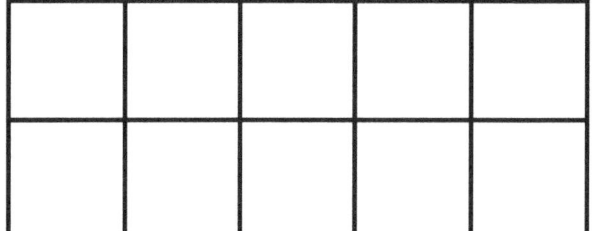

Equation

Answer

whales

COLOR BY SUM

Solve the addition problems. Use the color code to color the picture.

1= orange	4= green	7= red
2= black	5= blue	8= purple
3= gray	6= yellow	9= white

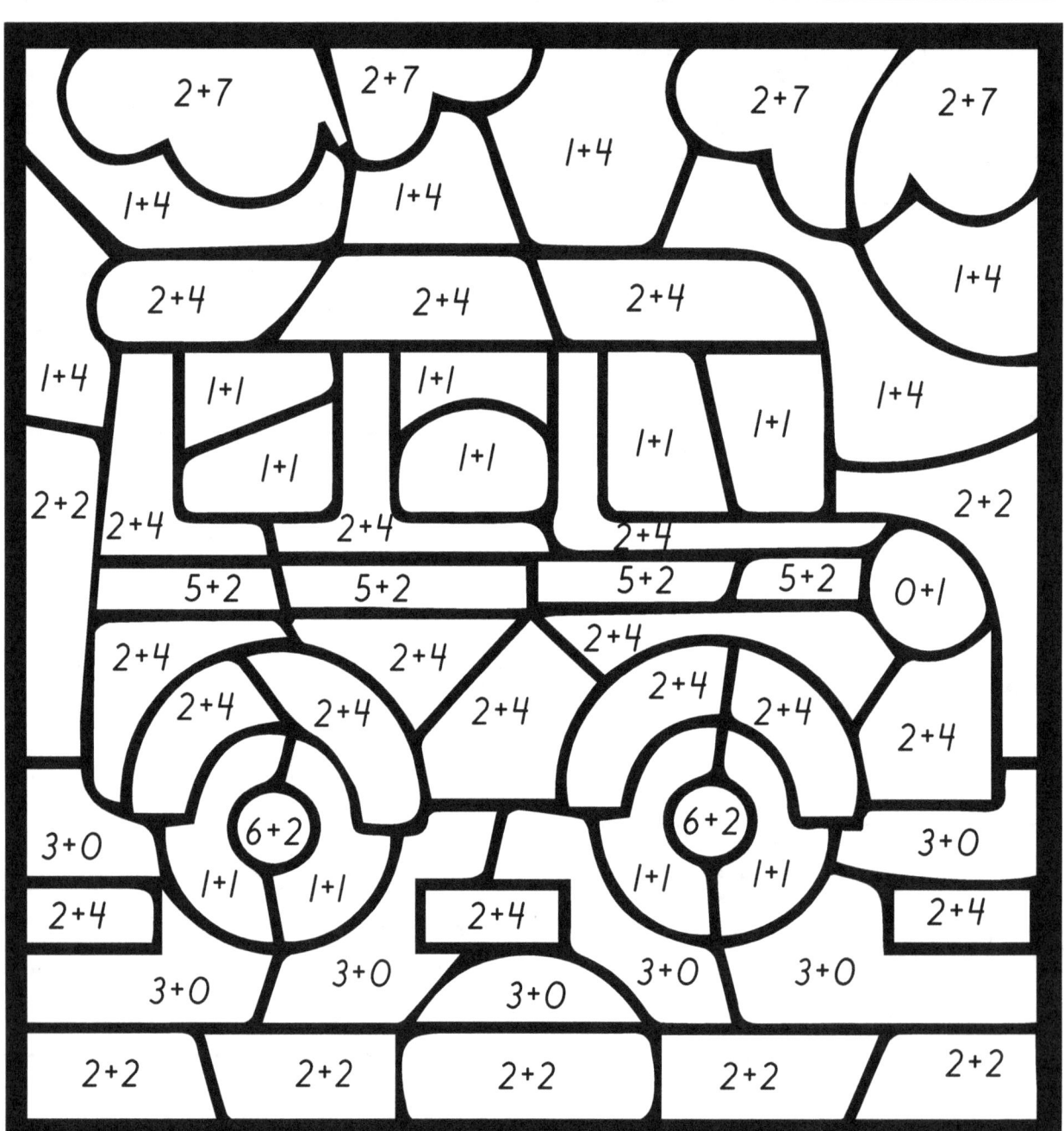

SUBTRACTION

BUG SUBTRACTION

Count and color the bugs in the jar. Place an X on the bugs to take away. Write the difference.

10 −2	10 −6	10 −4
10 −3	10 −7	10 −1
10 −2	10 −4	10 −5

FISH SUBTRACTION

Count and color the fish in the bowl. Place an X on the fish to take away. Write the difference.

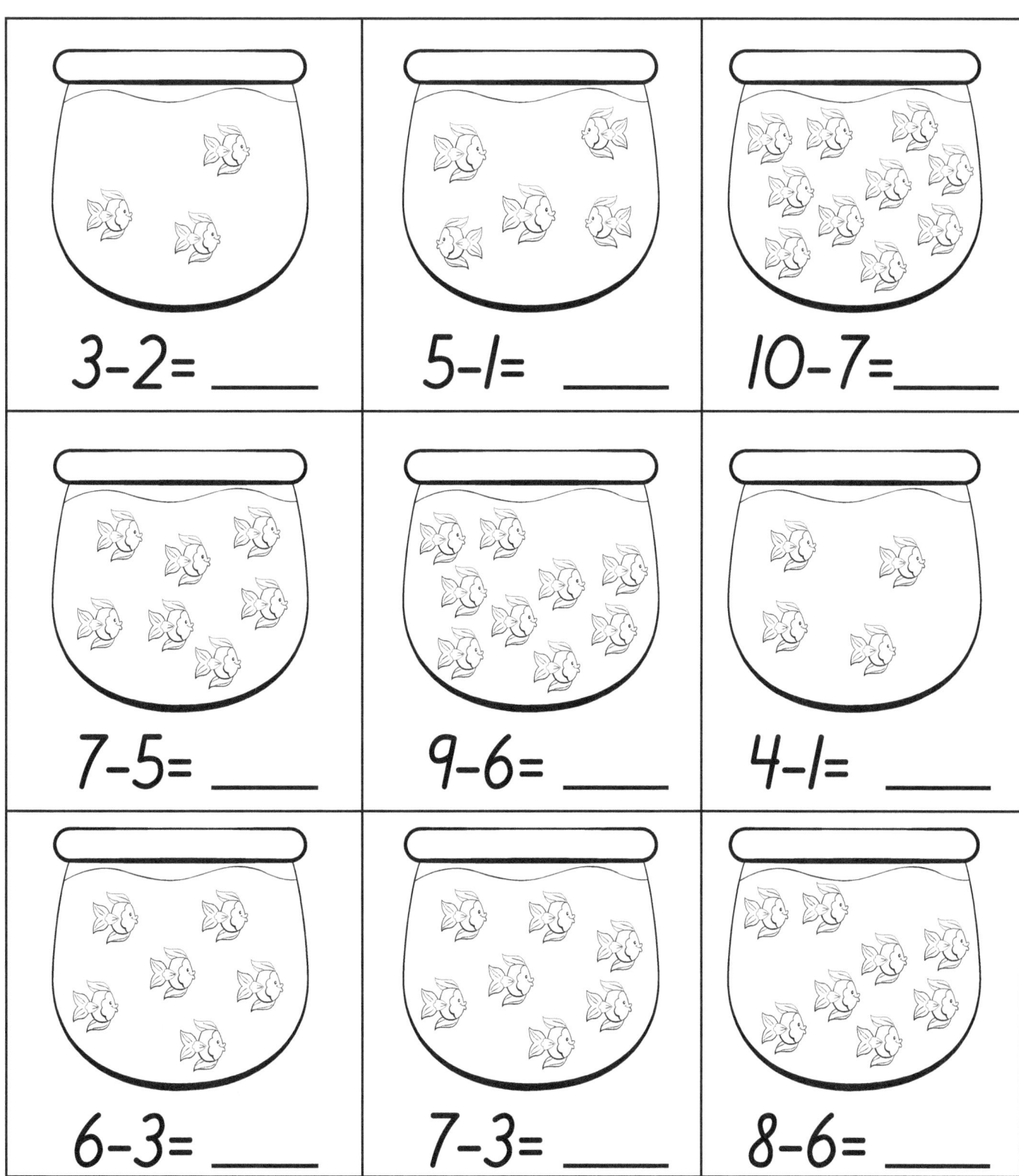

TEN FRAME SUBTRACTION

Read the equation. Start at the bottom, right-hand box and place an X in the box to take away. Write the difference.

10 – 2 =

10 – 6 =

10 – 5 =

10 – 8 =

10 – 3 =

10 – 9 =

10 – 7 =

10 – 4 =

NUMBER LINE SUBTRACTION

Place a dot on the number line for the top number of the equation. Then jump to the left to take away the bottom number of the equation. Circle the answer.

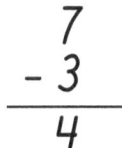
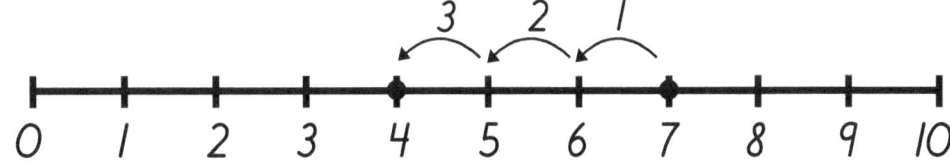

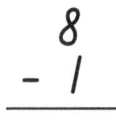
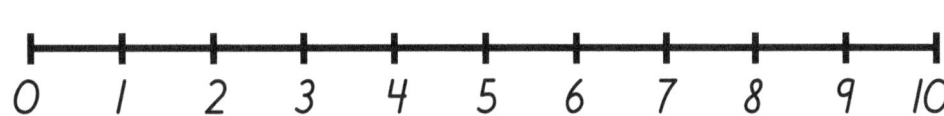

```
  5
- 4
```
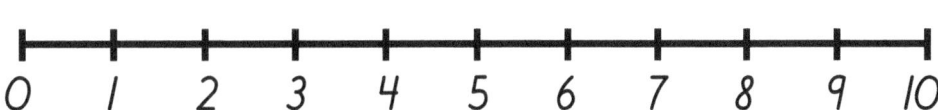

```
  7
- 2
```

```
  4
- 4
```

```
  6
- 5
```
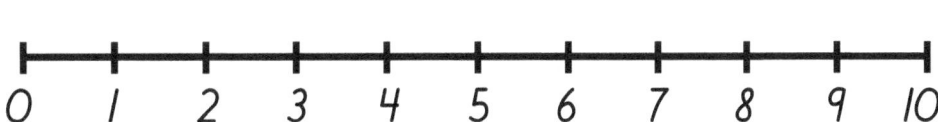

```
  3
- 1
```

```
  9
- 6
```
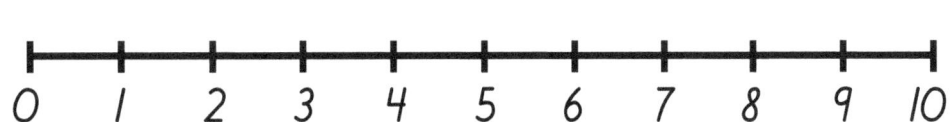

Learning Kindergarten Math Workbook | Autumn McKay

COLOR THE BUNNY

Solve the equations. Use the color code to color the bunnies.

4: yellow   5: blue   6: pink   7: purple

FIND THE ANSWER

Subtract. Color the box with the correct answer.

6 - 2 = | 5 | 8 | 4 |

10 - 1 = | 9 | 7 | 4 |

8 - 5 = | 5 | 6 | 3 |

4 - 2 = | 3 | 1 | 2 |

9 - 6 = | 3 | 4 | 7 |

7 - 3 = | 0 | 5 | 4 |

4 - 2 = | 7 | 6 | 2 |

6 - 4 = | 1 | 2 | 8 |

2 - 2 = | 0 | 1 | 2 |

SPORT SUBTRACTION

Solve the sports subtraction problems by crossing out the balls to be subtracted. Write the answer on the line.

6 - 2 = _____

8 - 5 = _____

4 - 3 = _____

5 - 1 = _____

7 - 4 = _____

8 - 3 = _____

10 - 6 = _____

FROG SUBTRACTION

Count and color the frogs on the log. Place an X on the ones to take away. Write the difference.

7 - 5 = ___

5 - 5 = ___

2 - 1 = ___

10 - 4 = ___

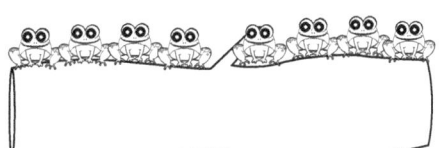

8 - 6 = ___

4 - 1 = ___

6 - 3 = ___

9 - 4 = ___

3 - 2 = ___

BEACH SUBTRACTION

Find the difference. Color the pictures.

```
  8      6      4      9      7
- 2    - 3    - 3    - 5    - 4
___    ___    ___    ___    ___


 10      5      6      3      8
- 5    - 2    - 4    - 1    - 5
___    ___    ___    ___    ___


  2      9      7
- 2    - 3    - 3
___    ___    ___
```

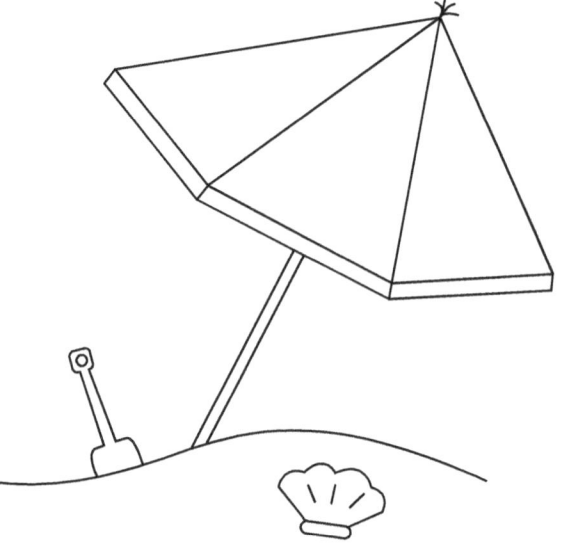

COLOR BY DIFFERENCE

Solve the subtraction problems. Use the color code to color the picture.

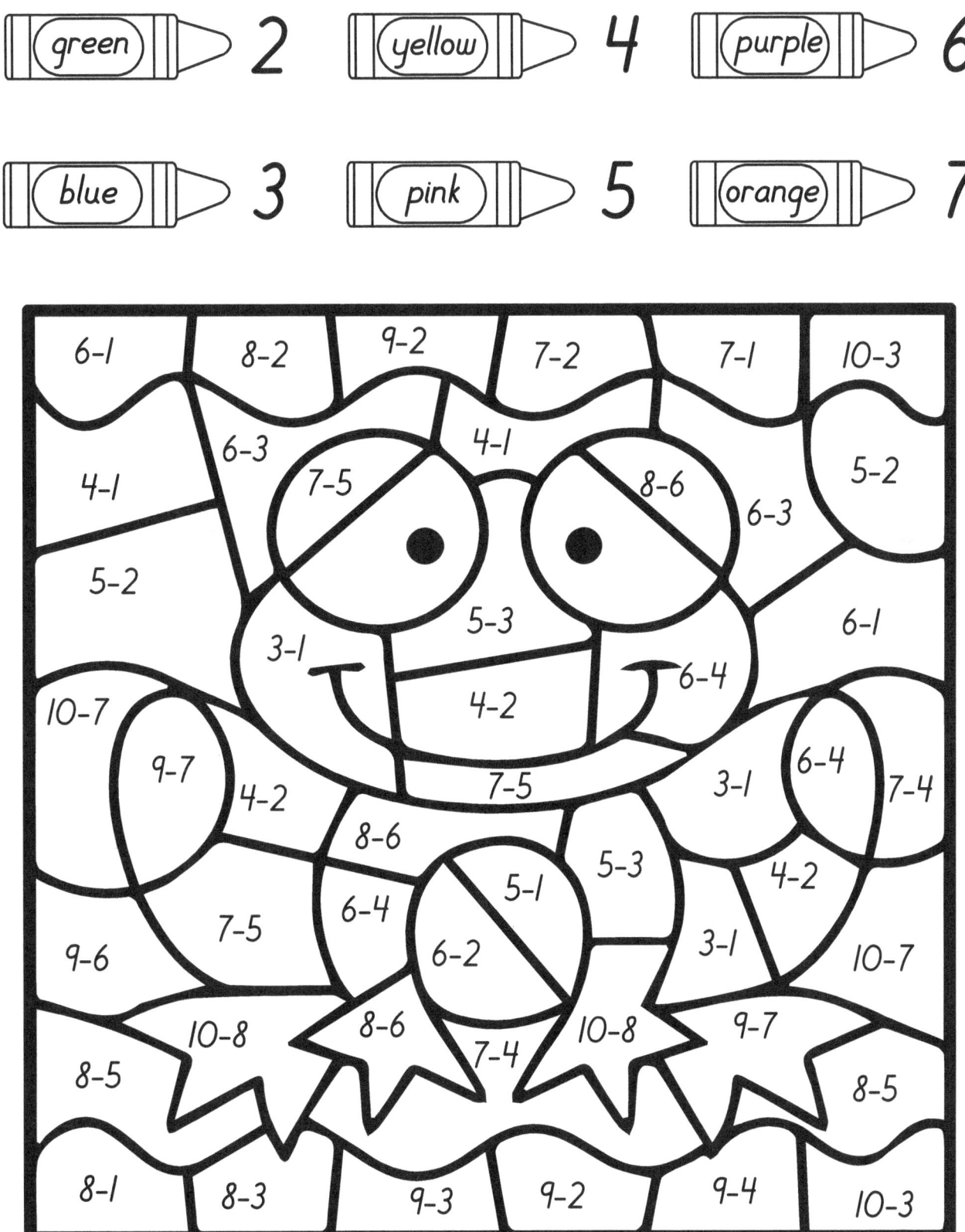

Learning Kindergarten Math Workbook | Autumn McKay

MEASURING

MEASUREMENT

Use the color code to color the picture to what each item measures.

length — red
width — yellow
temperature — blue
time — orange
volume — green

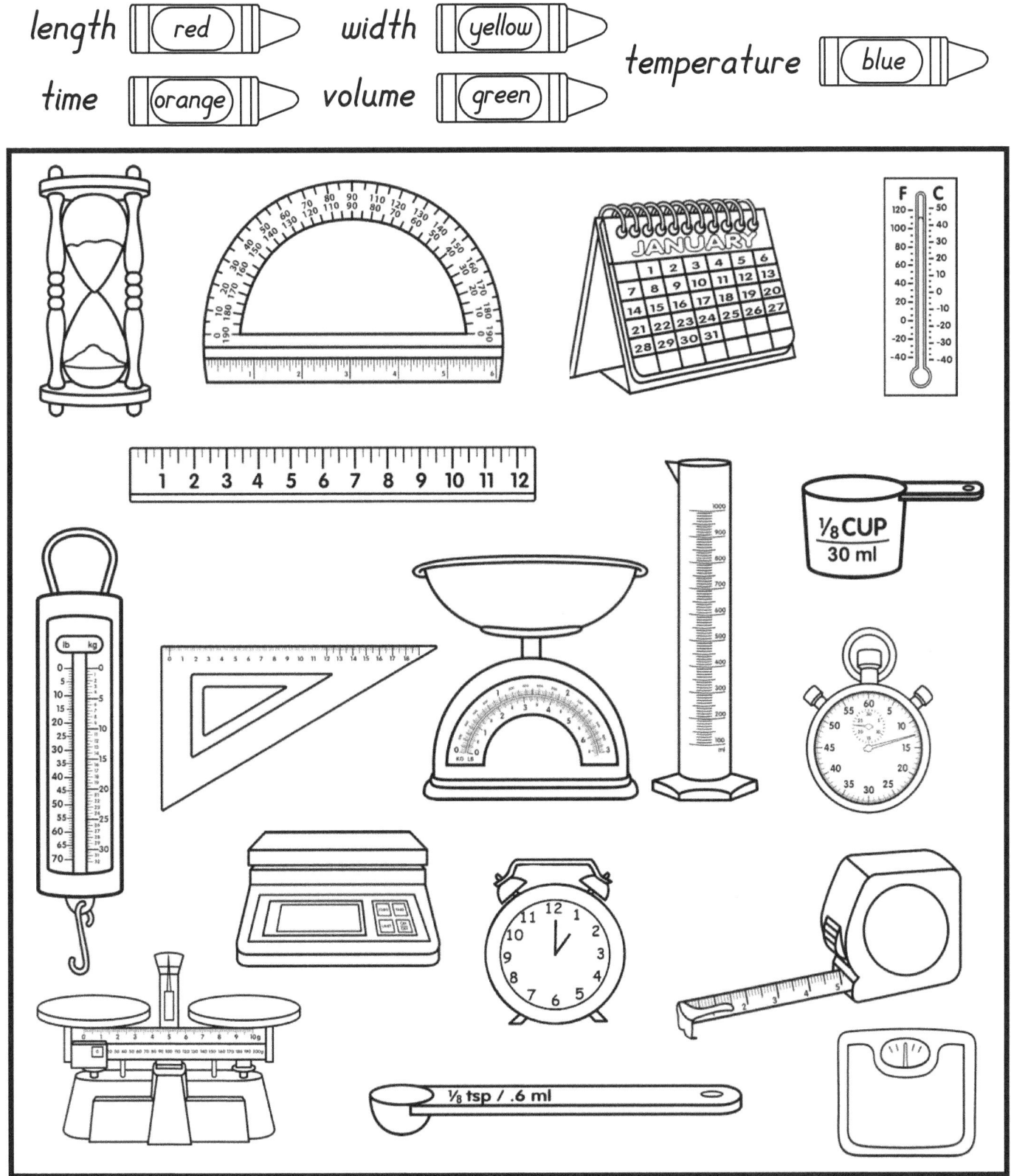

Learning Kindergarten Math Workbook | Autumn McKay

MEASURE THE ALLIGATOR

Count the number of blocks long each alligator measures.

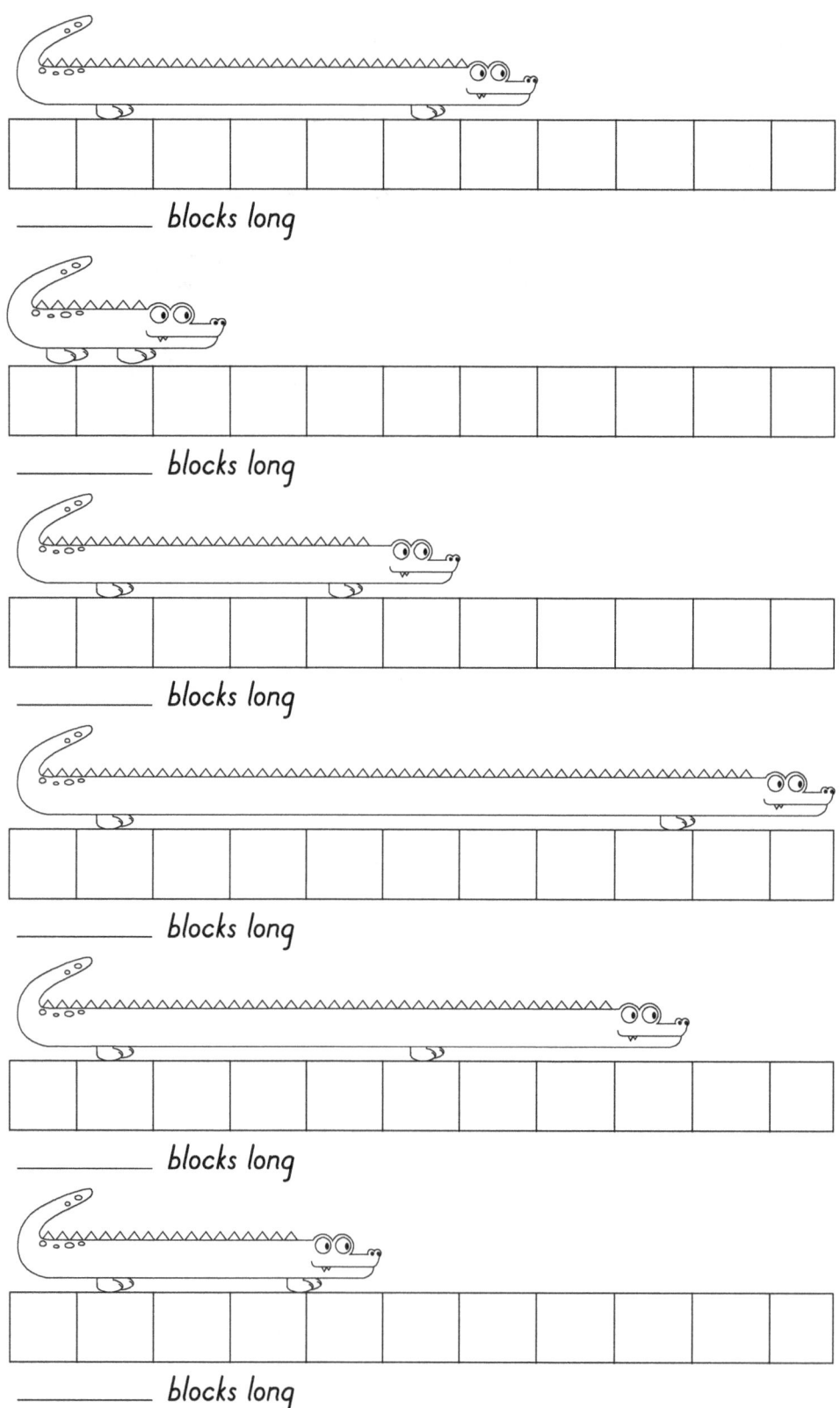

_____ blocks long

_____ blocks long

_____ blocks long

_____ blocks long

_____ blocks long

_____ blocks long

MEASURE THE ICE CREAM

Color the blocks to show the height of each ice cream cone.

BUGGY MEASUREMENTS

Measure the length of each bug using the ruler.

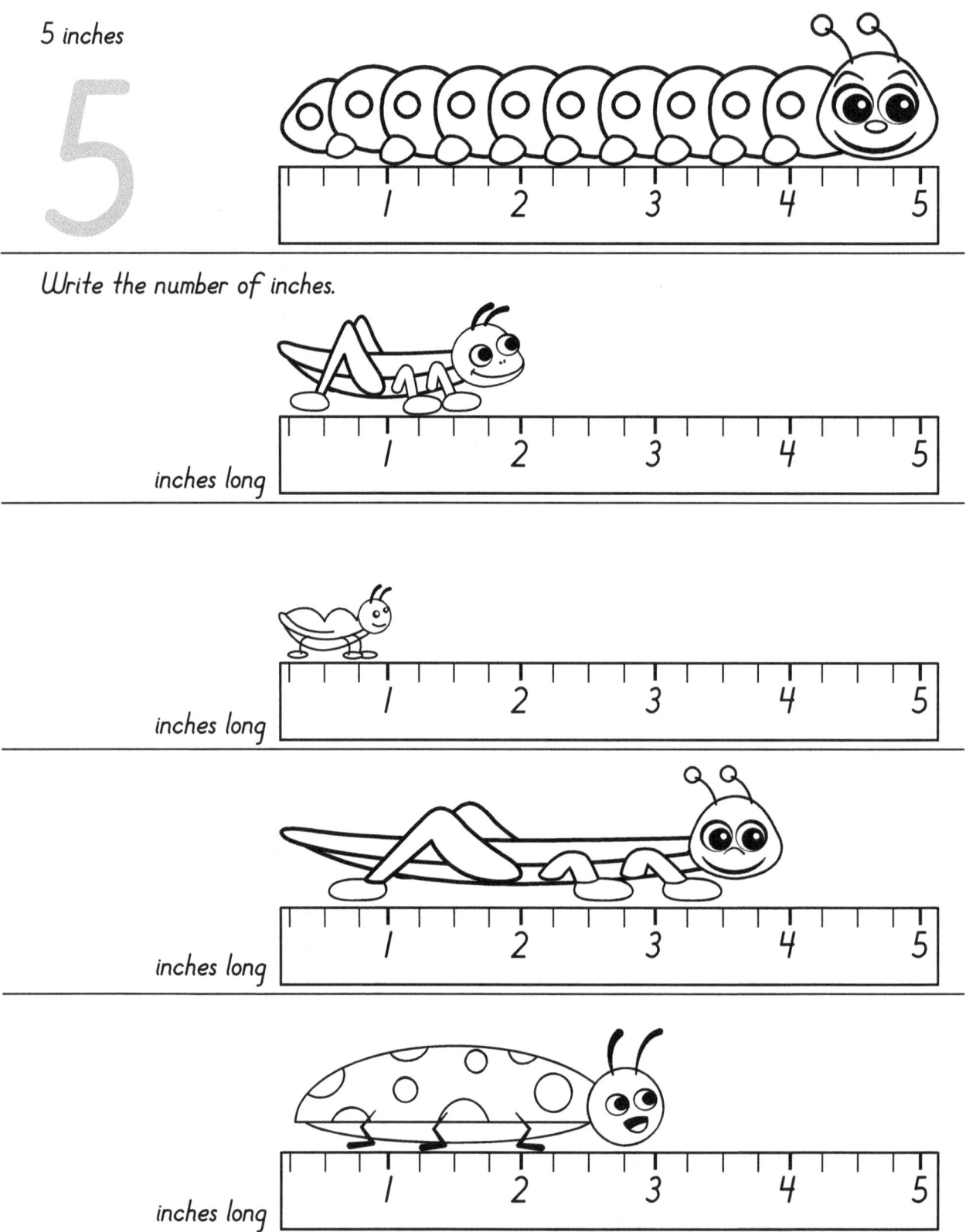

5 inches

Write the number of inches.

____ inches long

____ inches long

____ inches long

____ inches long

WHICH IS HEAVIER?

Look at the pictures in each box. Color the picture that is heavier.

CAPACITY MESUREMENT

Read the word under each container. Color the container with the correct amount.

CAPACITY SORT

In each row: Color the container that holds the most green. Color the container that holds the least purple. Color the container that holds a medium amount orange.

INCHWORM MEASURING

Cut out the inchworm ruler at the bottom of the page. Measure the length of each pencil to the nearest inchworm and write the answer.

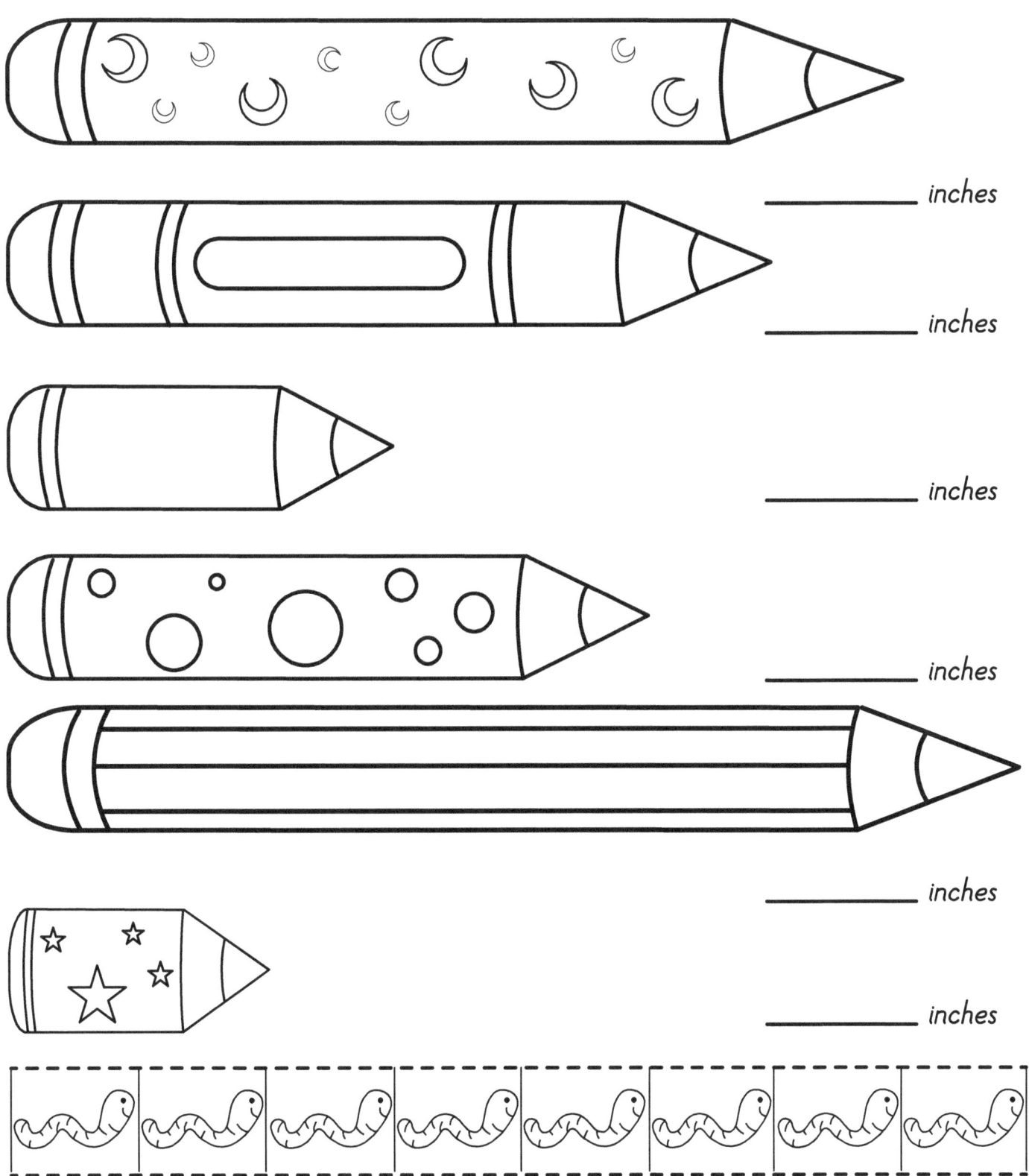

_____ inches

_____ inches

_____ inches

_____ inches

_____ inches

_____ inches

GARDEN MEASUREMENT

Use any form of a measuring tool (ruler, goldfish, paperclips, etc.) to measure each object. Write your answer in the box.

CROOKED MEASUREMENTS

Use a ruler to measure the crooked lines. Add the measurements together to see how long the line is.

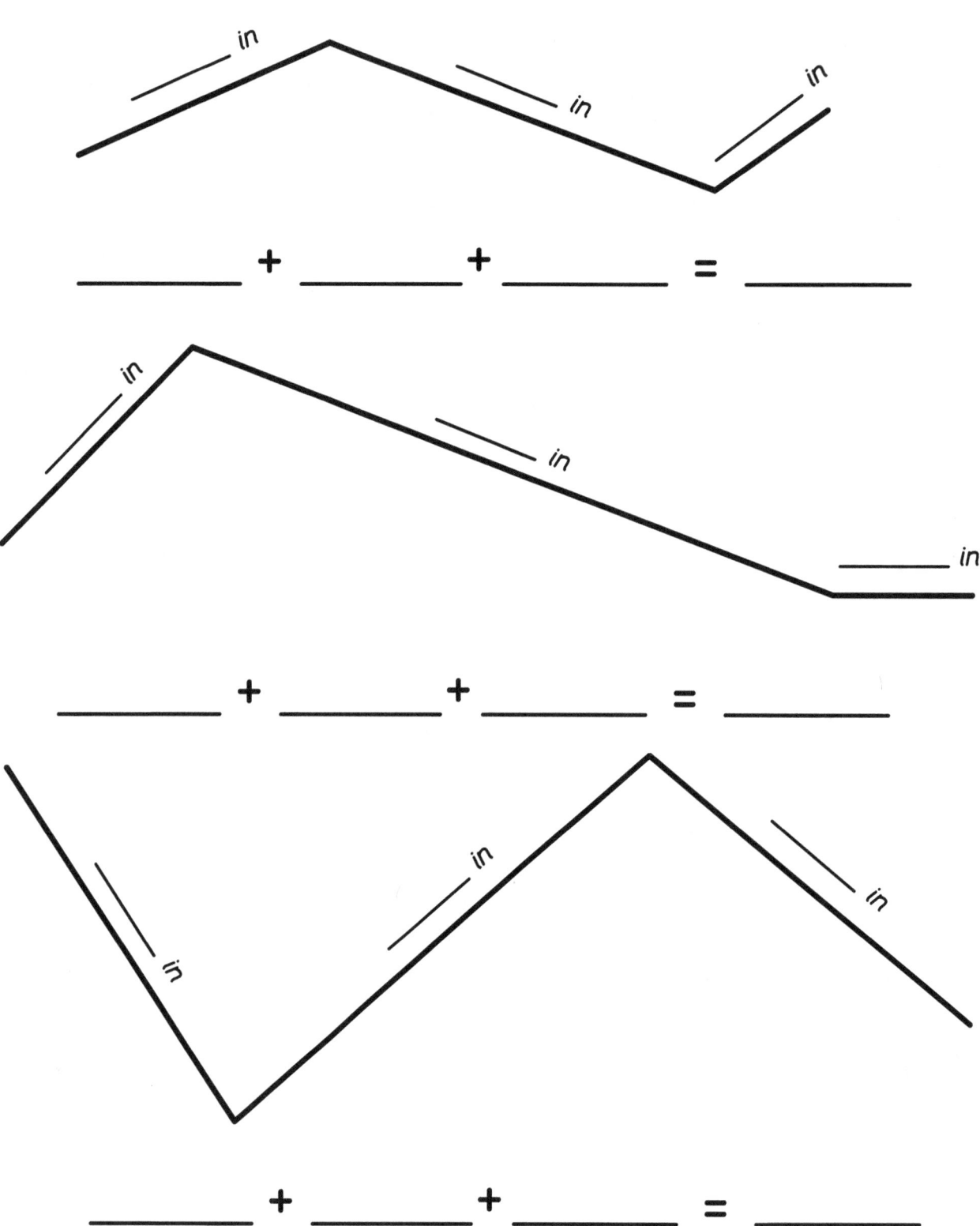

SHAPES

SHAPES

Color the shapes. Trace the shape's name.

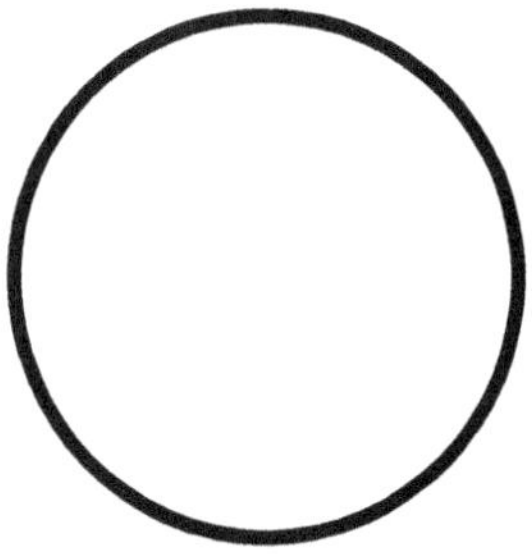

circle

star

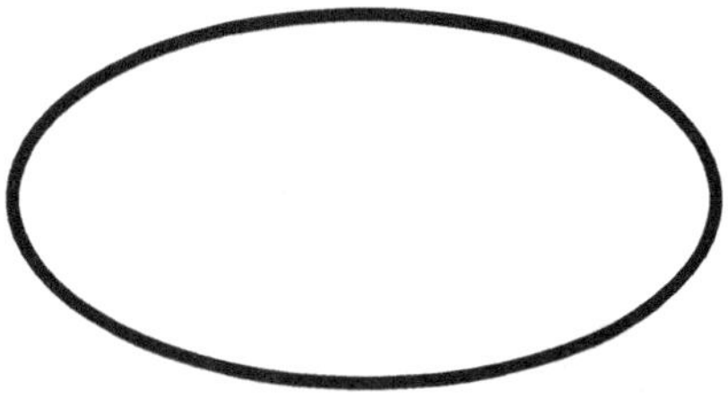

oval

rectangle

square

heart

TRACE THE SHAPES

Start at the dot and follow the arrows around the shape to trace it.

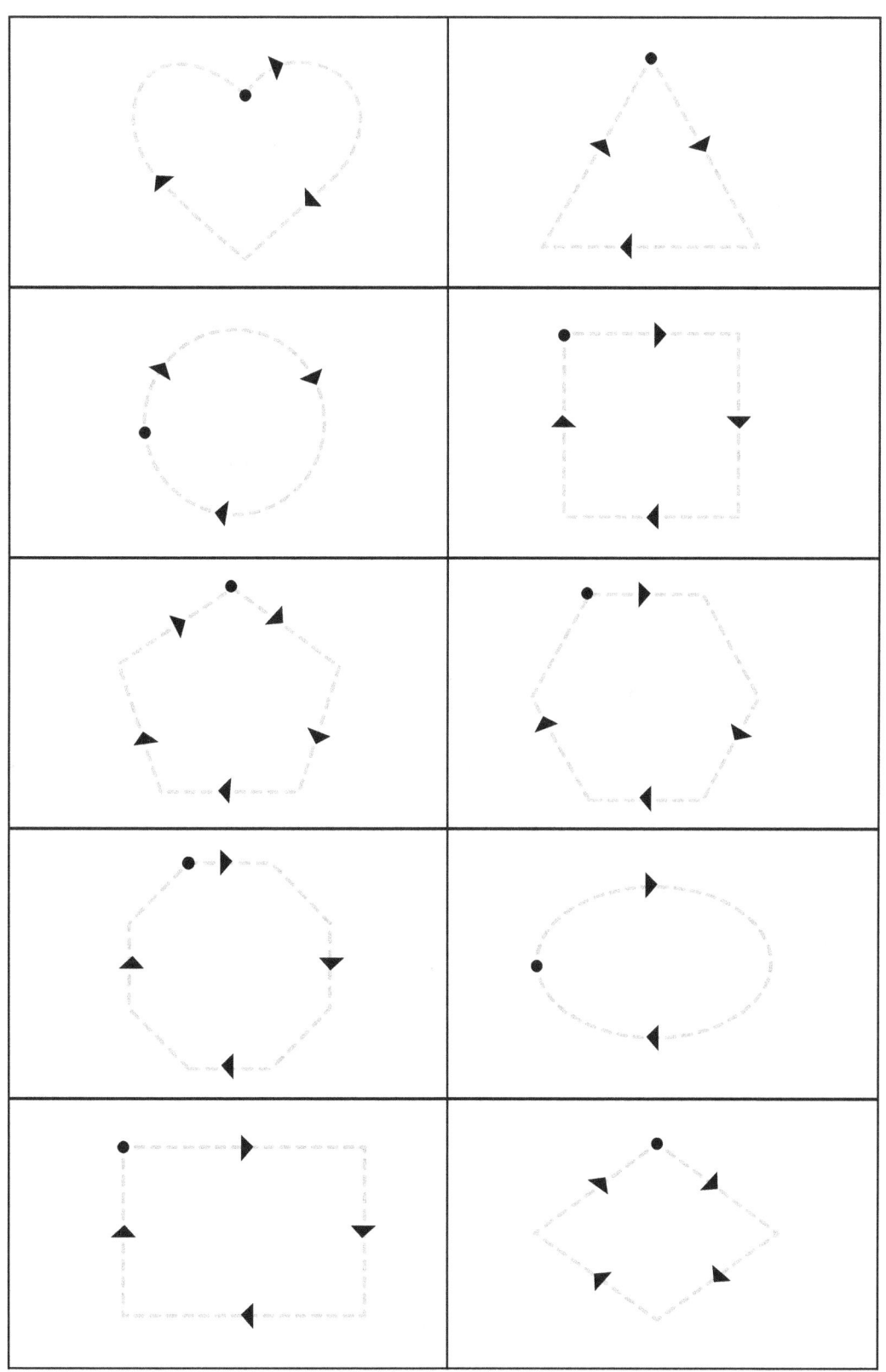

NUMBER OF SIDES

Count the sides of each shape. Use the code to color the shapes.

SHAPE CORNERS

Color the correct number of corners of each shape.

GRAPH THE SHAPES

Color the same shapes the same color. Count each shape. Graph the correct number of each shape.

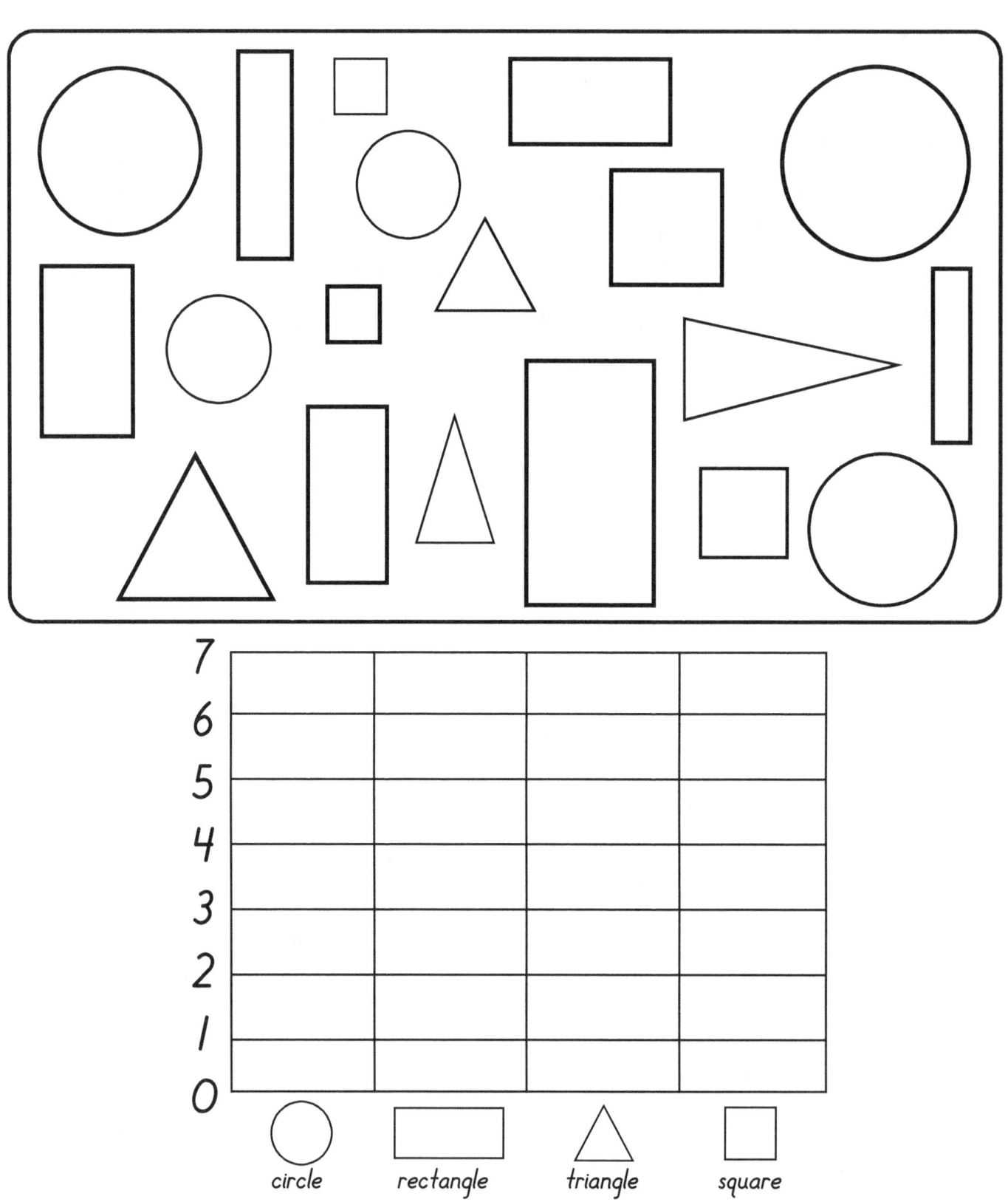

GUESS MY SHAPE

Use the clues to help you guess the 2D shapes. Once you determine the shape, draw it in the box.

I have 4 sides. Each side is equal. What shape am I?	I have 0 corners and 0 sides. I am a round shape. What shape am I?
I have 3 sides and 3 corners. What shape am I?	I have 4 sides and 4 corners. Two sides are long and the other two are short. What shape am I?

3D SHAPES

Color the shapes. Trace the shape's name.

sphere

cube

triangular prism

cone

pyramid

cylinder

2D OR 3D

Color the shapes according to the color code.

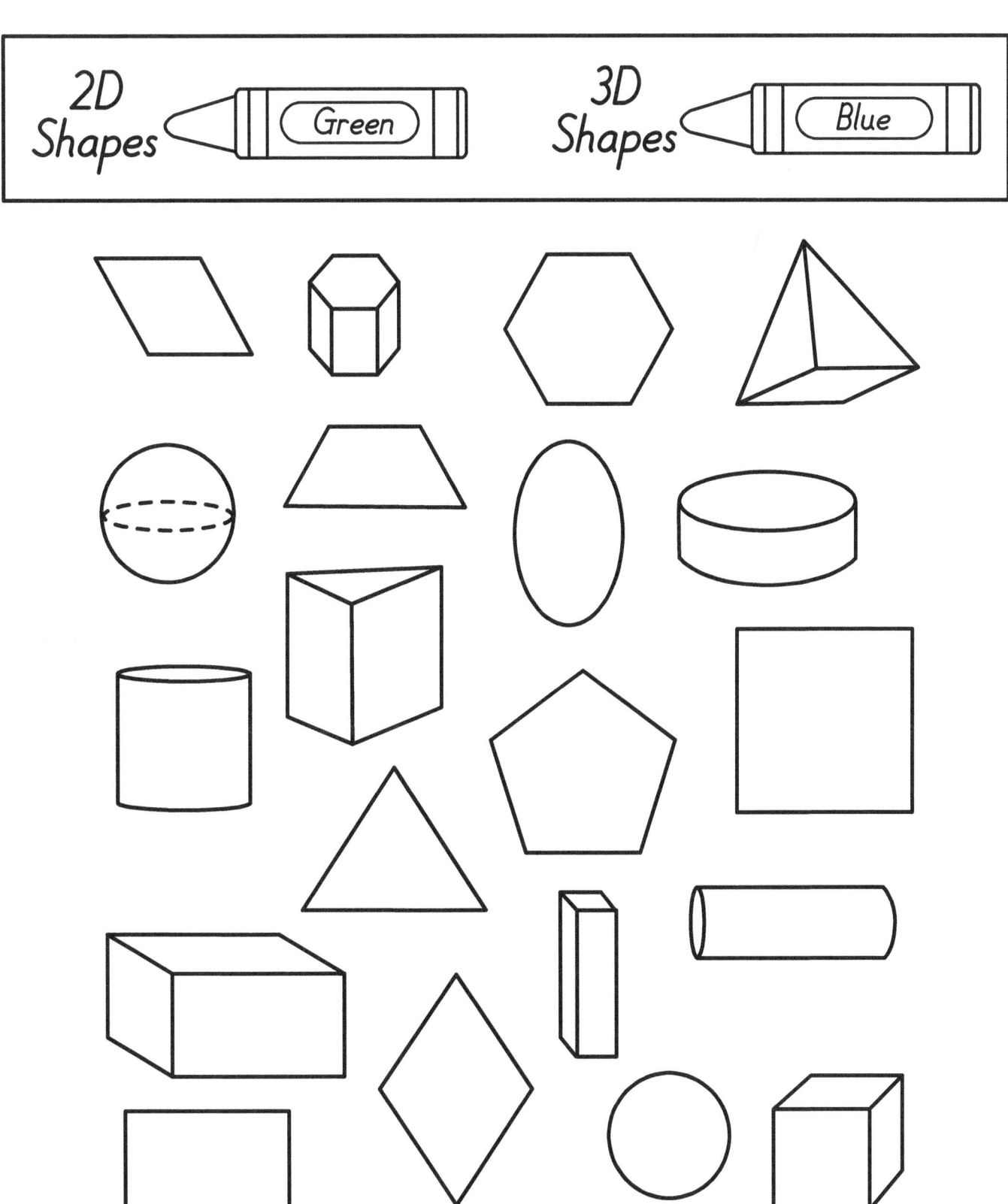

COLOR BY 3D SHAPE

Color the objects according to the 3D shape color code.

ROLL TO COLOR

Roll the die. Color one 3D shape for each die roll. See which shape fills up first!

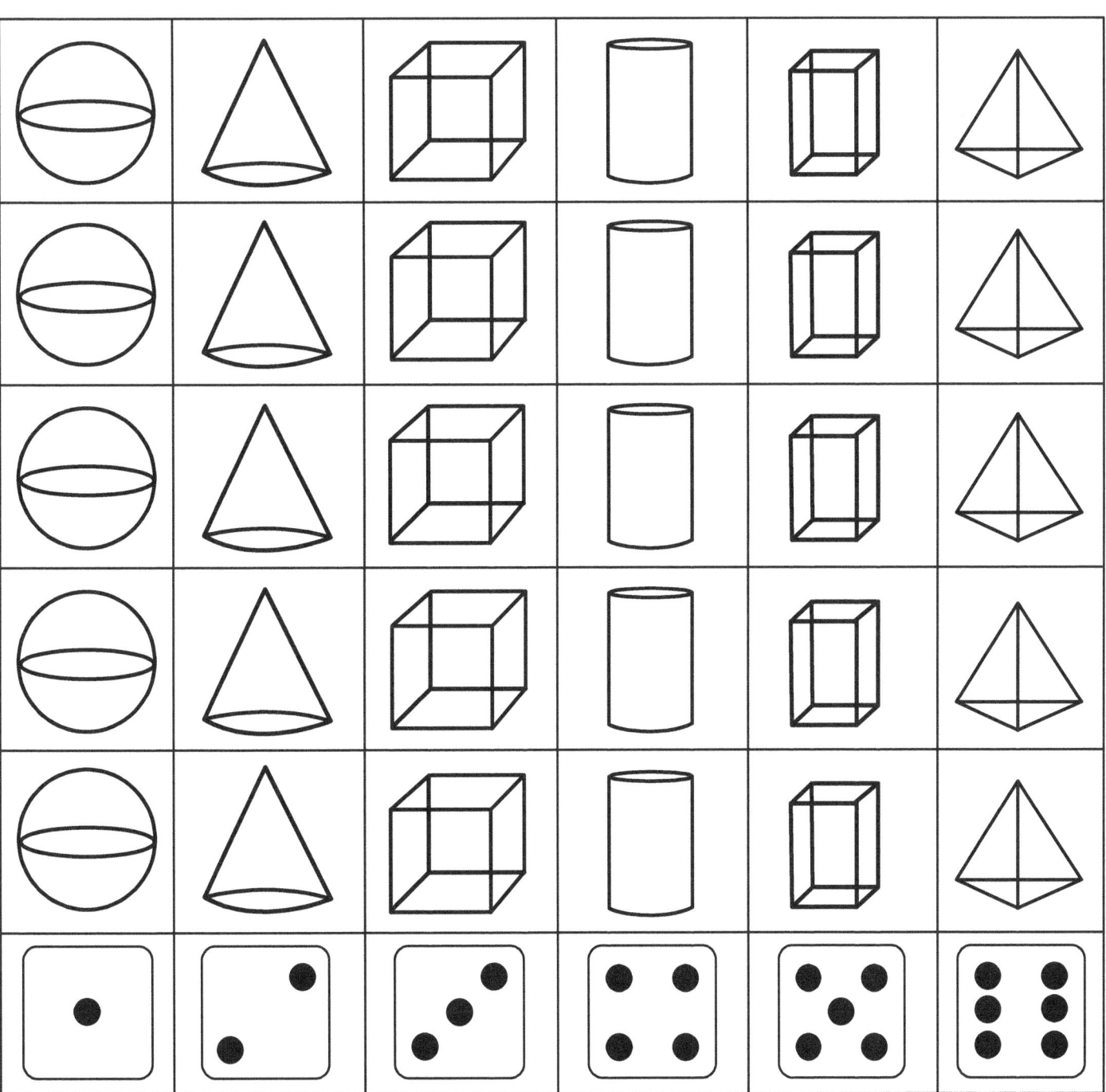

CALENDAR

MONTHS OF THE YEAR

Trace the months of the year. Color the pictures.

WRITE THE MONTHS

October July May November January December June March August September April February

• List the months in the correct order.

1. _____
2. _____
3. _____
4. _____
5. _____
6. _____
7. _____
8. _____
9. _____
10. _____
11. _____
12. _____

What month is it now? _____

How many months are there in the year? _____

When is your birthday? _____

What is the date today? _____

How many days are there in a week? _____

WHAT'S THE NEXT MONTH?

Read the months on each train car. Write the name of the next month in the last train car.

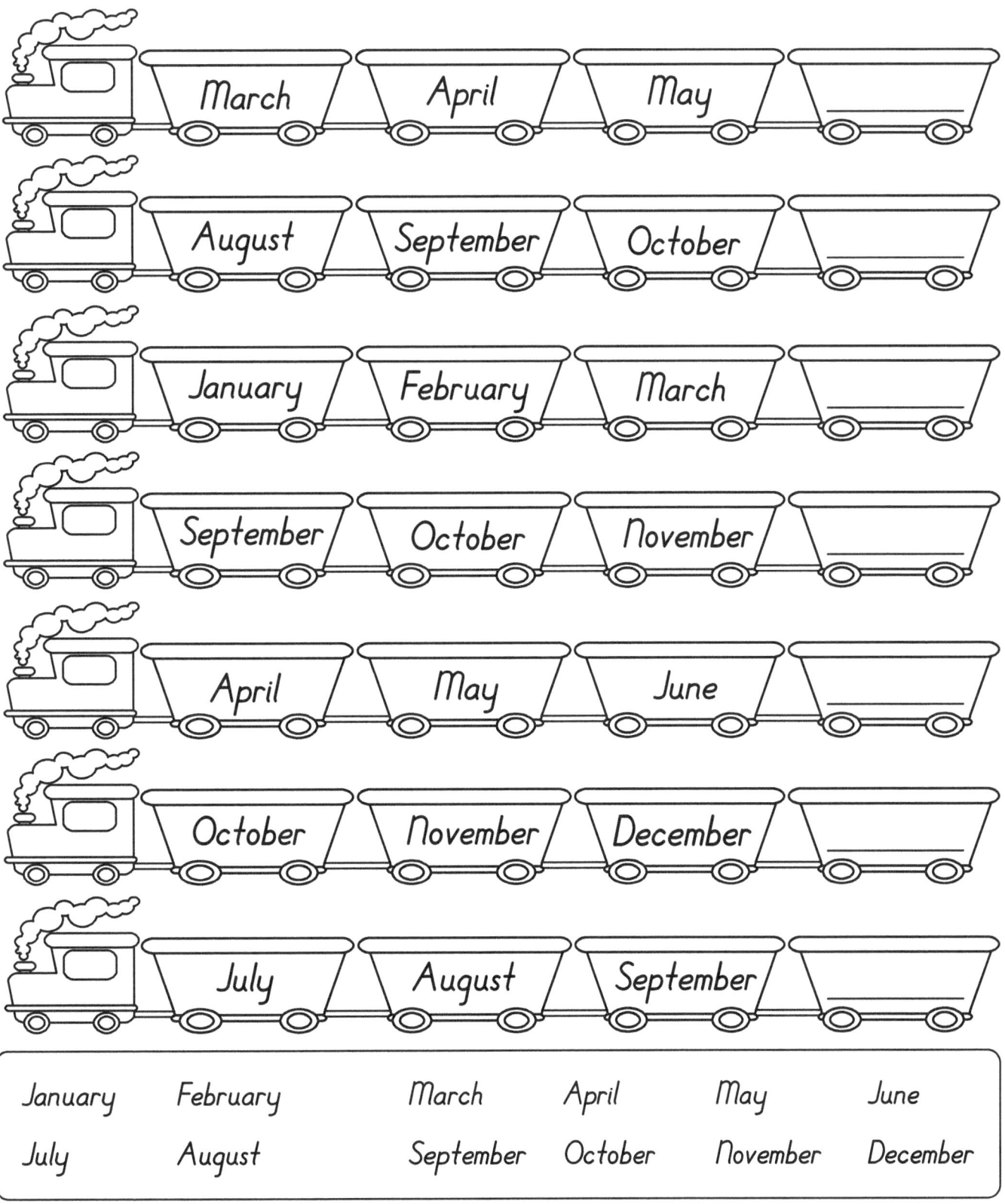

| January | February | March | April | May | June |
| July | August | September | October | November | December |

DAYS OF THE WEEK

Read the days of the week. Color the rainbow.

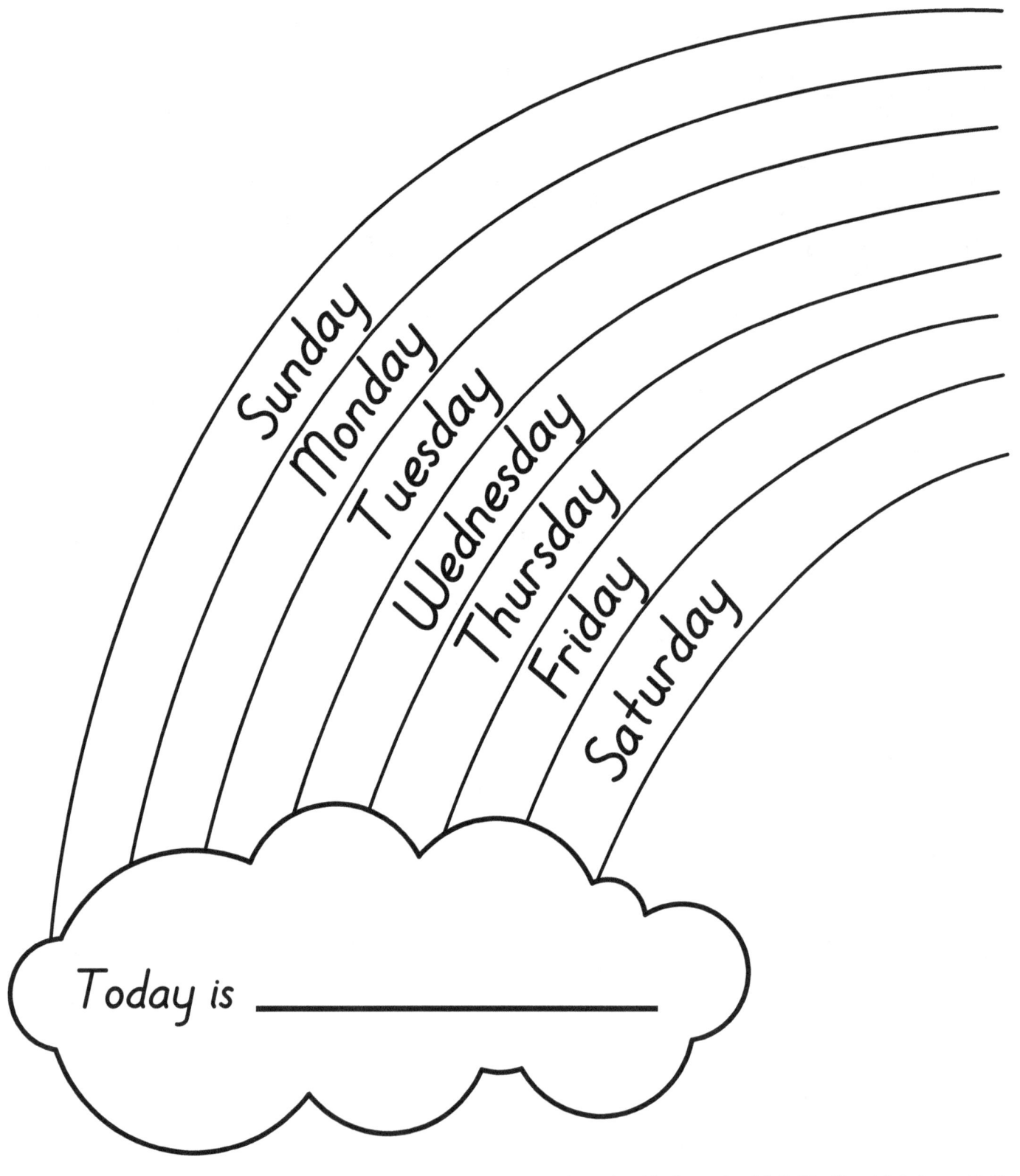

FILL IN THE BLANK

Write the missing letters to complete the spelling of the days of the week.

S ___ n ___ a ___

___ ond ___ y

Tu ___ ___ d ___ y

W ___ dn ___ s ___ ay

T ___ ur ___ d ___ y

Fr ___ da ___

S ___ t ___ ___ day

| Sunday | Monday | Tuesday | Wednesday |
| Thursday | Friday | Saturnday | |

WHAT'S NEXT?

Read the days on each train car. Write the name of the next day in the last train car.

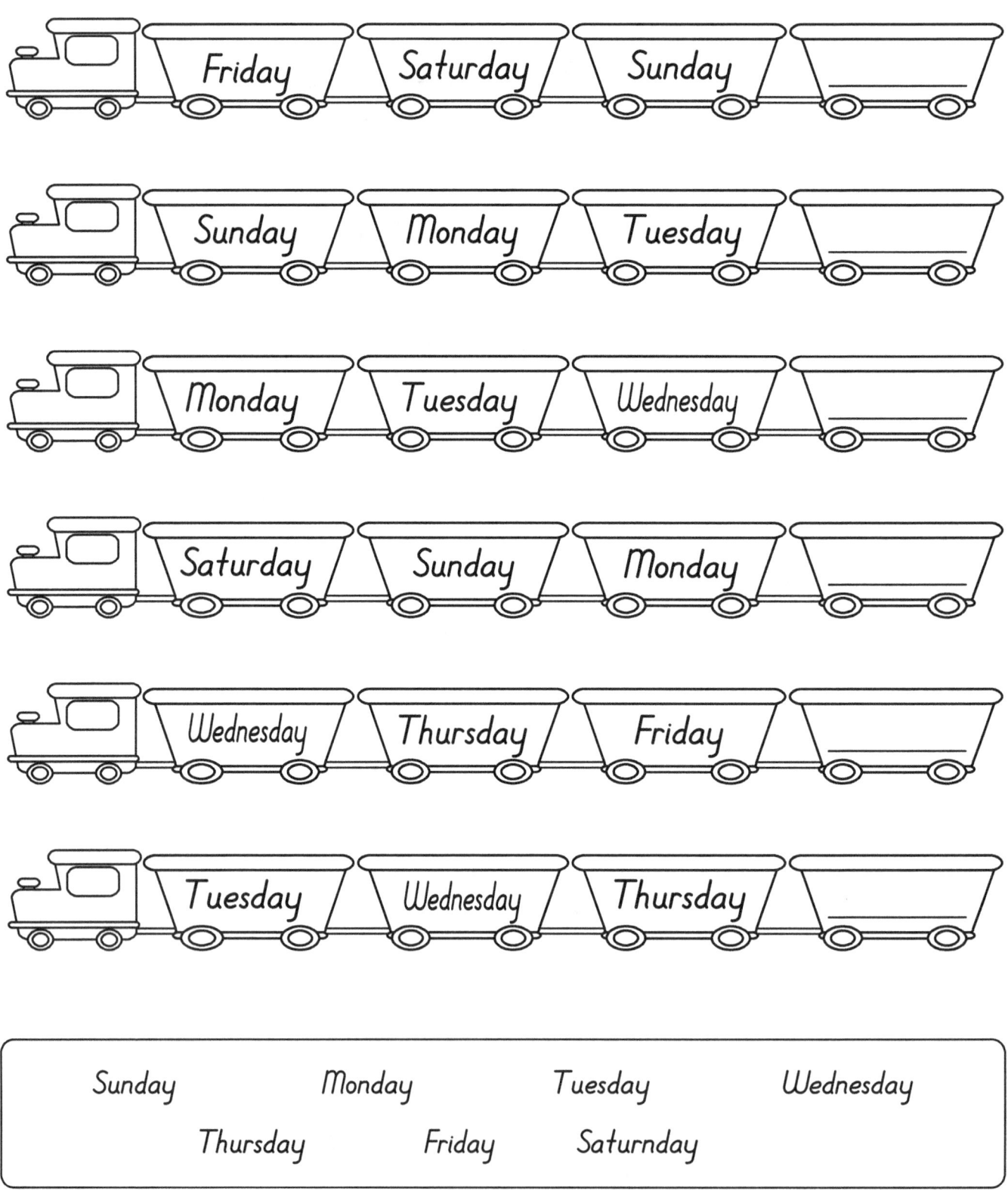

TODAY IS...

Write the month on the line.

_____

Color the Day

| Sunday | Monday | Tuesday | Wednesday | Thursday | Friday | Saturday |

Write the Date

Color the Weather

Color the Date

1	2	3	4	5	6	7	8	9	10
11	12	13	14	15	16	17	18	19	20
21	22	23	24	25	26	27	28	29	30
31									

TODAY IS... 2

Fill in each box with the correct information.

Circle the day

Sunday   Monday   Tuesday   Wednesday   Thursday   Friday   Saturday

| Month | Day | Year |

| yesterday was | tomorrow will be |

CALENDAR FUN

Use the calendar to answer the questions.

JUNE

Sunday	Monday	Tuesday	Wednesday	Thursday	Friday	Saturday
1	2	3	4	5	6	7
8	9	10	11	12	13	14
15	16	17	18	19	First Day of Summer 20	21
22	23	24	25	26	27	28
29	30					

1. Trace the name of the month with a red crayon.

2. How many days are in the month? _____

3. Write the name of the first day of the month. _____

4. When is the first day of summer? Month ____ Day ____ Year _____

5. Color all of the Mondays. How many Mondays are in the month? _____

Learning Kindergarten Math Workbook | Autumn McKay

CALENDAR

Color the day of the week.

| Sunday | Monday | Tuesday | Wednesday | Thursday | Friday | Saturday |

Color the month.

| January | February | March | April | May | June |
| July | August | September | October | November | December |

The day is?

_____

_____

The weather is?

The year is?

20____

WORD PROBLEMS

HOW MANY CHICKENS?

Read and solve the problem. Use all the ways to help solve the problem.

On the farm there are 3 brown chickens and 5 white chickens. How many chickens are there altogether?

Draw it.

Use the number line to solve the problem.

0 1 2 3 4 5 6 7 8 9 10

Color the boxes to solve the problem.

Write an equation to solve the problem.

_____ + _____ = _____

HOW MANY SHELLS?

Ben finds 8 seashells. Three seashells fell out of his bucket though. How many seashells does Ben have left?

Draw a picture.

Use a number line.

0 1 2 3 4 5 6 7 8 9 10

Write the equation.

____ - ____ = ____

Write the answer.

____ shells.

HOW MANY CUCAKES?

Read and solve the problem. Use all the ways to help solve the problem.

Susie brought 10 cupcakes to school to share for her birthday. She gave each of classmates a cupcake. She has 9 classmates. How many cupcakes does Susie have left?

Draw it.

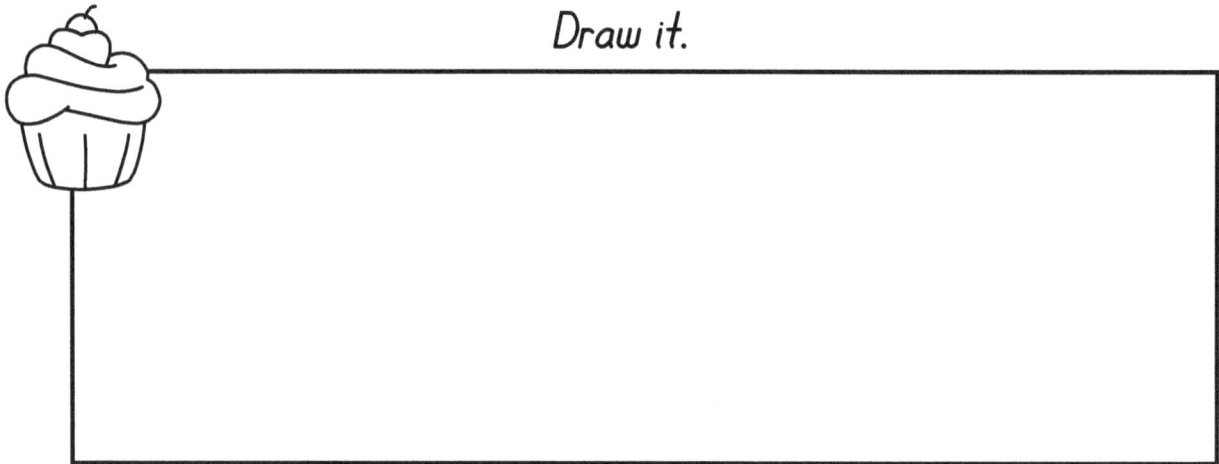

Use the number line to solve the problem.

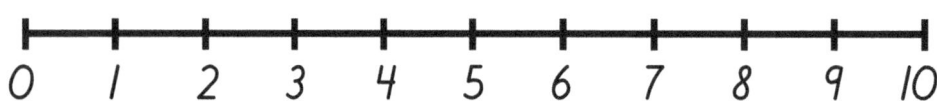

Color the boxes and cross out to solve the problem.

Write an equation to solve the problem.

_____ - _____ = _____

HOW MANY BIRDS?

A bird sits on her nest with 5 eggs. Two of the eggs have hatched. How many eggs still need to hatch?

Draw a picture.

Use a number line.

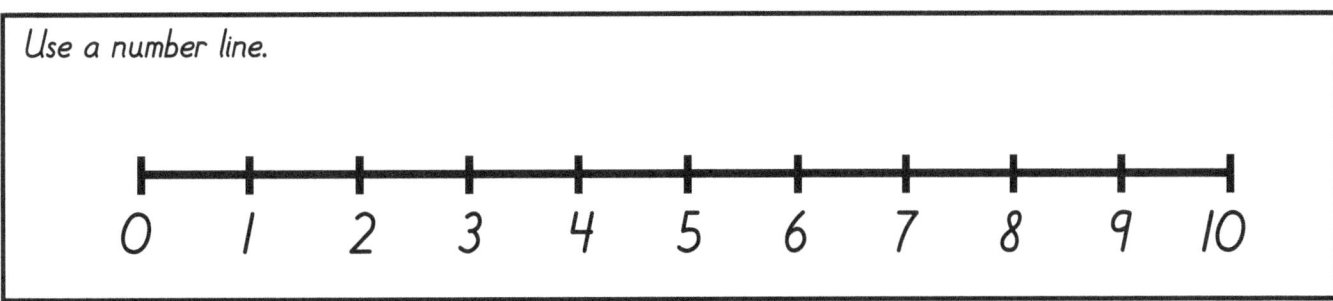

Write the equation.

____ - ____ = ____

Write the answer.

____ birds.

HOW MANY PETS?

Meg has 3 cats. Tom has 3 dogs.
How many pets are there in all?

Draw a picture.

Write the equation.

___ + ___ = ___

Write the answer.

_____ pets.

HOW MANY HORSES?

There were 7 horses at the stable. Four horses trotted to the pond. How many horses are at the stable now?

Draw a picture.

Write the equation.

___ - ___ = ___

Write the answer.

_____ horses.

HOW MANY ACORNS?

A squirrel started collecting acorns for winter. He found 4 acorns on Monday. He found 2 acorns on Tuesday. He found 3 acorns on Wednesday. How many acorns did he find altogether?

Draw a picture.

Write the equation.

___ + ___ + ___ = ___

Write the answer.

_____ acorns.

HOW MANY CRAYONS?

There are 5 crayons in the crayon box. There are 5 crayons on the table. John puts the 5 crayons from the table inside the box.
How many crayons are in the box now?

Draw a picture.

Write the equation.

____ + ____ = ____

Write the answer.

_____ crayons.

HOW MANY BEES?

There are 8 bumblebees on a flower. Two bumblebees fly away. How many bumblebees are still on the flower?

Draw a picture.

Write the equation.

____ - ____ = ____

Write the answer.

_____ bees.

HOW MANY PENNIES?

Alex had 9 pennies.
He spent 7 pennies on a piece of candy.
How many pennies does Alex have left?

Draw a picture.

Write the equation.

____ - ____ = ____

Write the answer.

_____ pennies

Congratulations!

You have successfully completed your Learning Kindergarten Math Workbook!

Don't forget to claim your completion certificate. Scan the QR code or visit this link: www.bestmomideas.com/learning-kindergarten-math-certificate

Certificate of Completion

This Certifies That

_____

Has Successfully Trained & Completed the

LEARNING KINDERGARTEN MATH WORKBOOK

You can graduate to the
Learning 1st Grade Math Workbook!

Parent/Guardian Signature: _____   Date: _____

Thank you for welcoming me in your home! I hope you and your child liked learning together with this book!

If you enjoyed this book, it would mean so much to me if you wrote a review so other moms can learn from your experience.

Autumn@BestMomIdeas.com

Discover Autumn's Other Books

Early Learning Series

Early Learning Workbook Series

www.BestMomIdeas.com   @BestMomIdeas   Best Mom Ideas

www.ingramcontent.com/pod-product-compliance
Lightning Source LLC
Chambersburg PA
CBHW081751100526
44592CB00015B/2383